W9-BSP-062

DATE DUE

CESAR
CHAVEZ

CESAR CHAVEZ

Jeff C. Young

MORGAN REYNOLDS

PUBLISHING

Greensboro, North Carolina

american workers

The Homestead
Steel Strike of 1892

The Pullman Strike of
1894

The Ludlow Massacre
of 1913-14

Mother Jones

Cesar Chavez

CESAR CHAVEZ

Copyright © 2007 by Jeff C. Young

Library of Congress Cataloging-in-Publication Data

Young, Jeff C., 1948-
   Cesar Chavez / by Jeff C. Young.
      p. cm.
   Includes bibliographical references and index.
   ISBN-13: 978-1-59935-036-3 (library binding)
   ISBN-10: 1-59935-036-X (library binding)
   1. Chavez, Cesar, 1927---Juvenile literature. 2. Labor leaders--United
States--Biography--Juvenile literature. 3. Mexican
Americans--Biography--Juvenile literature. 4. Migrant agricultural
laborers--Labor unions--United States--Officials and
employees--Biography--Juvenile literature. I. Title.
   HD6509.C48Y68 2007
   331.88'13092--dc22
   [B]
                                          2006025973

Printed in the United States of America
First Edition

To Manuela Davila, who worked in the fields.

CONTENTS

Cesar Chavez
(Courtesy of Time Life Pictures/Getty Images)

CHAPTER 1.

Highest Honor

The United States can bestow no higher honor on a civilian that the Presidential Medal of Freedom. Cesar Chavez received that honor, a year after his death, on August 8, 1994, when President Bill Clinton presented the medal to his widow, Helen.

In his address, the president lauded the noted labor leader and advocate of nonviolence: "Cesar Chavez, before his death in April of last year, had become a champion of working people everywhere." President Clinton remarked that Chavez "rose to become one of our greatest advocates of nonviolent change." He concluded his brief remarks

Cesar Chavez led the fight for better pay and working conditions for migrant farmworkers. (Courtesy of Time Life Pictures/Getty Images)

by reminding his audience of how Chavez had led a movement to improve the living and working conditions of thousands of the United States' migrant farmworkers who made their living by following the crops from place to place in an annual cycle of planting, cultivating, and harvesting:

The farmworkers who labored in the fields and yearned for respect and self-sufficiency pinned their hopes on this remarkable man, who, with faith and discipline, with soft-spoken humility and amazing inner strength, led a very courageous life. And in so doing, brought dignity to the lives of so many others, and provided for us inspiration for the rest of our nation's history.

The life story of Cesar Chavez is now an integral part of the history of California's agricultural industry. Even

President Bill Clinton awarded Chavez a posthumous Medal of Freedom.

before California became a state, wealthy landowners exploited the poor, who were often immigrants with little education, to harvest their crops. For more than a century, California farmers kept wages for farmworkers low by pitting one group of poor workers against others competing for work.

The early Spanish settlers in California used the local Indians to toil in their fields, often under slave-like conditions. Then the Gold Rush that began in 1849 drastically changed the demographic makeup of California when more than 250,000 prospectors, mostly Anglos from the U. S., rushed in hoping to strike it rich panning for gold. When only a few got rich, thousands found themselves stranded and jobless.

When California became the thirty-first state in 1850 it was isolated from most of the other population centers of the U.S. until Congress agreed to fund the building of a transcontinental railroad. In order to save money, the builders of the railroad in California hired Chinese immigrants to lay the tracks. After the railroad was completed, resentful small farmers, who could not compete with large farmers using the Chinese as a cheap labor force, frequently harassed the often industrious and thrifty Chinese. This situation eventually led to the passage of the Chinese Exclusion Act of 1882, which banned more Chinese from immigrating to the United States for ten years and barred U.S. courts from granting citizenship to Chinese immigrants already living in the United States.

But the demand for cheap labor could not be stopped so easily. Soon Japanese immigrants began to replace the

Chinese laborers were first imported into California to help build the Central Pacific Railroad during the 1860s. (Library of Congress)

Chinese as a source of cheap, dependable labor, which led to more resentment and discrimination. The Japanese had brought superior farming methods to America and soon began acquiring and cultivating land that other farmers had not been able to make productive, which created even more tension. Over time, the backlash against the Japanese grew so strong that the U. S. Congress passed the Alien Land Act of 1913. It kept the Japanese and other immigrants from acquiring more farmland.

Early in the twentieth century more cheap labor began to come into the state from the south. The Mexican Revolution of 1910 created thousands of refugees who came across the border illegally. The Mexicans were easier to take

A dust storm approaches Stratford, Texas, in 1935. (National Oceanic & Atmospheric Administration)

advantage of because the farmers could threaten them with deportation if they asked for higher wages or better working conditions. The Mexican labors were further disadvantaged when, during the 1920s, large farmers began importing workers from the Philippines. The Filipinos were usually willing to work for even lower wages than the Mexicans.

The Great Depression, along with the drought conditions that led to the Dust Bowl in Texas, Oklahoma, and Arkansas during the 1930s, created a new wave of desperate, displaced farmers swarming into California willing to work cheap. Now that there was a surplus of available workers, efforts were stepped up to keep Mexicans from crossing the southern border.

There were some movements in the U.S. to help workers. The passage of the landmark National Labor Relations Act (NLRA) in 1935 improved working conditions and job security for millions of workers. The law established the right to form and join labor unions and to engage in collective bargaining with employers for higher wages and improved working conditions. However, the law excluded farmworkers from its protections.

Some Mexican farmworkers formed unions and engaged in strikes anyway, but most of the unions were not able to survive. There were too many unemployed looking for work for them to sustain a meaningful strike. The growers created their own organization, the Associated Farmers of California to stop workers from forming unions.

During the 1940s and 1950s migrant farmworkers began attempting to organize into unions to demand better pay and working conditions. (Courtesy of Walter P. Reuther Library, Wayne State University)

Mexican migrant workers, called braceros, being trucked to the fields during harvesttime. (Courtesy of Walter P. Reuther Library Wayne State University)

When the United States entered World War II in 1941, the surplus of cheap workers began to dry up as millions either enlisted or were drafted into the armed forces. Most of those who were not physically fit for military service were not equipped for the hard manual labor of harvesting crops.

Suddenly, the farm owners needed workers. A series of agreements with the Mexican government made migrant Mexican farmworkers welcome in the United States again. Mexican field hands known as braceros were trucked into

California and other southwestern states at harvesttime. After the harvest ended, they were quickly trucked back to Mexico. World War II changed the labor situation in California forever. Enough workers had seen the benefits they were able to gain if they worked together against the powerful farmers. Soon after the war a labor organizer named Ernesto Galarza began organizing farmworkers in California's Central Valley into the National Farm Labor Union (NFLU). While Galarza was able to get the workers to join the NFLU, he was not able to get their employers to recognize and negotiate with the union. From 1947 to 1950, the NFLU was on strike against DiGiorgio Farms, California's largest grower of produce, but the strike failed.

The NFLU was eventually replaced by the Agricultural Workers Organizing Committee (AWOC). The AWOC had the backing of America's largest collection of labor unions, the American Federation of Labor and Congress of Industrial Organizations (AFL-CIO), but that was not enough to ensure its success. It would be the 1960s before migrant farmworkers were finally able to force the growers to recognize their right to collective bargaining and union contracts. This change came about largely because of the untiring efforts, determination, and dedication of Cesar Chavez.

CHAPTER 2.
Arizona to California

When Cesar Chavez was born in Arizona his ancestors had lived in the area for more than forty years, but many people regarded the Chavez family as Mexican instead of American.

Cesar's grandfather, Cesario, came to the United States in the 1880s. He had worked on a large hacienda in Chihuahua, Mexico where the economic conditions of the workers were similar to those on an American plantation before the Civil War. "On the hacienda, they were slaves," Chavez said. "The moment a baby was born, they would give him a tag and start keeping a book on him of all his expenses. By the time the child grew old enough to start working, he was already sold, he already owed a lot of money."

Chavez's grandfather escaped from a hacienda in Chihuahua, Mexico, where he was held under armed guard, to come to the United States. (Library of Congress)

In addition to economic enslavement, the hacienda owners had another method of keeping their workers in line. The owners had an arrangement with the Mexican government to draft their workers into the army if they dared to defy or disagree with them.

When Cesario found himself in this situation he escaped the hacienda and crossed the Mexican border into El Paso, Texas. There, he got a job working for the railroad, and he also worked as a farmworker. He lived frugally and was able to save enough money to bring his wife and fourteen children to America. Sometime around 1888, Cesar's father, Librado, came to America.

The Chavezes settled near Yuma, Arizona. Cesario acquired some horses and mules and started a hauling business serving Yuma, Gila Bend, and other Arizona mining

After his escape from Mexico, Cesar's grandfather worked cutting firewood during the building of the Laguna Dam near Yuma, Arizona. (U.S. Department of the Interior)

towns. When the federal government began building the Laguna Dam, Cesario got a contract for cutting firewood and hauling it to the construction site. The steady income allowed him to build an adobe house, dig some irrigation ditches, and begin farming and homesteading on around one hundred acres of land sometime around 1909.

On June 15, 1924, Cesar's father Librado married Juana Estrada. He was thirty-eight and she was six years younger. Where and when they met is not recorded. Juana was barely more than five feet tall and very talkative. Librado was nearly six feet tall and very quiet. They were two very different people, but they formed a loving and lasting partnership.

In 1925, Librado bought a business about a mile away from his father's farm that consisted of three buildings: a pool hall, a garage, and a small grocery store that also served as their home. Cesar Chavez was born there on March 31, 1927. He was the second of five children and was named for his grandfather, Cesario.

Librado worked hard to make his business a success, but he was not a good businessman. He was too generous and trusting. "My dad often blindly trusted people," Chavez recalled, "a trait that would get him and us into trouble many times later on."

Cesar's mother, Juana, was a devout Catholic and inspired Cesar to lead a life of nonviolence. She instructed her children with Mexican proverbs known as *dichos*. The nonviolent teachings she chose conflicted with another aspect of Mexican culture:

> Despite a culture where you're not a man if you don't fight back, she would say, 'No, it's best to turn the other cheek. God gave you senses like eyes and mind and tongue, and you can get out of anything.' She would say, 'It takes two to fight.' That was her favorite. 'It takes two to fight and one can't do it alone.'

Along with detesting violence, Juana, would not tolerate selfishness. "Although my mother opposed violence, I think the thing that she really cracked down on the most was being selfish," Cesar said. "She made us share everything we had. If we had an apple or a tiny piece of candy, we had to cut it into five pieces."

Cesar's oldest sister, Rita, was like a second mother. She was two years older than Cesar and babysat for him and his younger brother, Richard, while Juana helped on the family farm. Cesar's close relationship with Rita brought about his first public display of stubbornness and a willingness to defy authority. When he entered school, Cesar refused to sit with his first-grade classmates. He defiantly told his teacher that if he could not sit with his sister he was going home. Six-year-old Cesar tightly hugged Rita and began crying. After he was pried loose, he ran out of the building. Rita chased him down and convinced him to return to school.

When they returned, the teacher gave in and let Cesar sit at a desk next to his sister: "After two or three days—I can't remember how many—he finally agreed to go with the first graders, but he won that first battle then and there."

Despite that victory, Cesar never really liked going to school. He was smart and willing to learn, but often clashed with his teachers. "Getting to school was a big chore for me," Cesar said. "Unlike Rita, I never liked school. They made me go, so I went, but they always had to push me to go. It wasn't the learning I hated, but the conflicts. The teachers were very mean."

The primary conflict between Cesar and his teachers was language. Cesar was proud of his Mexican heritage and was accustomed to speaking Spanish. His teachers insisted that he speak English, but when he spoke English his accent caused him to mispronounce words, which greatly embarrassed him:

> Of course, we bitterly resented not being able to speak Spanish, but they insisted that we had to learn English. They said that if we were American, then we should speak the language, and if we wanted to speak Spanish, we should go back to Mexico. When we spoke Spanish, the teacher swooped down on us. I remember the ruler whistling through the air as its edge came down sharply across my knuckles. It really hurt.

Even speaking Spanish outside of the classroom would get them in trouble. If Cesar and his friends were caught speaking Spanish on the playground, the principal would spank them with a wooden paddle. "But I could take a spanking," Cesar recalled. "What was worse was mispronouncing a word or making a grammatical mistake. With my Spanish accent and background, I couldn't avoid that. I'd get embarrassed and that hurt more than a paddling. . . . It's a terrible thing when you have your own language and customs, and those are shattered."

Cesar's problems at school were soon overshadowed by economic problems brought on by the Great Depression. In late October 1929 the values of stocks fell far below the prices that investors had paid for them. Individual investors, banks, and businesses lost tens of millions of dollars. Thousands of banks and businesses closed. By 1933 nearly thirteen million Americans were unemployed, approximately 25 percent of the nation's workforce.

People gather on the subtreasury building steps across from the New York Stock Exchange in New York on "Black Thursday," October 24, 1929. Thousands of investors lost their savings in the worst stock market crash in Wall Street history on October 29, 1929, after a five-day frenzy of heavy trading. The Great Depression followed thereafter. (Courtesy of the Associated Press)

Because most of Librado's customers were family and friends he extended them credit. But when they could not pay their bills, the store went bankrupt. He moved his family into his father's old adobe house, where his widowed mother was living and he returned to farming to support his family. But a combination of harsh weather conditions and the lingering effects of the Great Depression doomed him to failure. Severe drought plagued the southwestern United States. In the past, the Colorado River had fed and filled the irrigation ditches on the Chavez homestead, allowing them to raise and sell corn, squash, watermelon and chilies. Now the ditches were dry and dusty, and the once fertile soil reverted to desert.

Librado was unable to even pay the property taxes on the family farm. Thanks to a federal program, Librado qualified for a loan to pay the $3,600 in back taxes, but a neighboring farmer who coveted the Chavezes' property was able to stop the loan. "The guy next to us who wanted the land was the president of the bank, and also of the soil conservation office, so the loan was blocked," Chavez remembered.

Librado's only hope of paying off the tax bill was to head west to California. He had heard that there were jobs for farmworkers there. He hoped to earn enough money to keep the family farm and, in August 1938, he left his family behind and headed north to California.

Librado found work in Oxnard, California, threshing beans. The hours were long and the pay was meager, but he felt lucky to have a job when there were so many Dust Bowl refugees looking for work. The surplus of available workers allowed the farm owners to keep the wages low. Librado found a small, rickety shack to live in and sent for his family. Juana, their five children and two of

Oxnard, California, as it looked when the Chavez family lived there. (Library of Congress)

The Colorado River (left) brings life to the desert surrounding Yuma, Arizona (right). (The National Archives; © Jason West)

Cesar's cousins all piled into an old Studebaker. On the second day of their trip, they were stopped and detained by the Border Patrol. For eleven-year-old Cesar, it was a frightening ordeal:

> Suddenly two cars bore down on us, their floodlights shattering the dark. Uniformed men piled out of the cars and surrounded ours. We were half-asleep, all scared and crying. Roughly, they asked for identification, our birth certificates, proof of American citizenship. They harassed my mother without mercy. She was terrified.

Juana could not speak English, and the only identification she had was a letter from Librado.

The Border Patrol officers accused the Chavezes of smuggling Mexicans across the border and leaving them in the desert. After five nerve-racking hours, the Border Patrol finally let them go.

Librado hoped the entire family would be able to work and make enough money to reclaim their farm. Monday through Friday, Cesar and his siblings attended school half of the day and helped their parents the rest of the day. On Saturdays and Sundays, the entire family worked picking walnuts. When the harvest season ended, they returned to Arizona.

Despite their hard work, the Chavezes had not made enough money to pay their tax bill. Librado refused to give up. He traveled to Phoenix and was able to speak to the governor. It did not help. On February 6, 1939, an advertisement appeared in the Yuma newspaper announcing that the Chavez family farm would be sold at a public auction.

Years later, Cesar recalled how difficult it was to lose what three generations of his family had worked so hard for:

> The ad said, the Yuma County Board of Supervisors would sell at public auction 118.58 acres, located in the North Gila Valley. It said nothing, of course of Papa Chayo, who plowed the land, irrigated it, and made it produce. Nor did it mention my dad who had continued the work and struggled there for the survival of his family. The ad made only one thing clear. The county now owned the land because the former owners failed to pay $4,080.80 due the county for taxes and seven years of interest on those taxes.

Librado made one final effort. At the public auction, there were only two bidders, Librado and a rich grower named Archibald Griffin. Griffin wanted the land because it was adjacent to land he already owned. Librado was the higher bidder with a $2,300 offer and the county gave him thirty days to come up with the money. But it was not to be. After Librado was turned down for a loan again, Griffin bought the property for $1,750.

Cesar's final memory of the family farm was watching everything his family had built, planted, and nurtured be systematically destroyed. He realized that his life would never be the same:

> A big red tractor came to the farm—at least it seemed big to me as my dad had always farmed the land with horses. Its motor blotted out the sound of crickets and bullfrogs and the buzzing of flies. As the tractor moved along, it tore up the soil, leveling it, and destroyed the trees, pushing them over like they were nothing. . . . They (the trees) are a part of you.
>
> We grew up there, saw them every day, and they were alive, they were friends. When we saw the bulldozer just uprooting those trees, it was tearing at us too.
>
> After pushing down the trees, the tractor destroyed the wooden gates of the carefully dug irrigation ditches. Then it headed for the farm's corral.
>
> Now the tractor was at the corral, and the old sturdy fence posts gave way as easily as stalks of corn. It was a monstrous thing. Richard and I were watching on higher ground. We kept cussing the driver, but he didn't hear us, our words were lost in the sound of tearing timbers

and growling motor. We didn't blame the grower, we blamed the poor tractor driver.

We just thought that he was mean. I wanted to stop him but I couldn't. I felt helpless.

It was time for the Chavez family to leave their land. They loaded up their old Studebaker with their few possessions and set out for California. For the next seven years, Cesar would come into adulthood working as a migrant farmworker.

CHAPTER 3.
Sal Si Puedes, Migrants

In California the Chavez family faced stiff competition for even the most menial farm jobs. By selling his cows and chickens, Librado had raised only forty dollars to support a family of seven. Clearly they needed to find work soon, but there were thousands of adults and children looking for the same jobs in California in 1939.

Librado heard that there was work picking peas available in the town of Atascadero. When he arrived, he learned that the harvest had ended several weeks earlier. Then he was told that there was work in Gonzales, one hundred miles farther north.

In Gonzales, the only affordable housing the Chavezes could find was a single room above a bar. The blaring jukebox kept them awake for most of the night. The next day, Librado met a labor contractor who told him there were good paying pea-picking jobs available near the small

During Cesar's early years working the fields, he and his family lived in several towns in California.

coastal town of Half Moon Bay. He gave Librado his card and told him whom to report to. Later, they learned the contractor was being paid twenty dollars for every family he recruited. When they reported for work, they found the wages were less than half of what the contractor had promised them. Since there was no other jobs available, they took the wages they were offered.

The Chavezes were accustomed to hard work, but this first pea-picking job taught them how badly migrant farm-workers were exploited. They were given hampers to fill with peas, and it took about two hours of backbreaking labor to fill them. They had to walk slowly down the rows of peas, doubled over to reach the crop. When their hamper was full they had to go to the end of a long line and wait

Both children and adults participated in the backbreaking labor of pea picking. Once each bushel basket was full, pickers brought them to be weighed. (Library of Congress)

to have the peas sorted and weighed. Any peas that did not pass inspection were thrown out. The pay was twenty cents a hamper, and the hamper had to weigh twenty-five pounds. In three hours, the entire family made only twenty cents. "After the weigh-in, we found there were no more hampers, no more work that day. There were so many unemployed people looking for jobs, they were like flocks of starlings," Cesar remembered.

While working picking peas, they rented a small house for four dollars a week. In order to live they had to spend more than they made. The work was too sporadic to provide them a steady income. Once again, Librado heard that there was work elsewhere. This time, it was in San Jose picking cherries.

In San Jose, most of the migrant farmworkers lived in a small, crowded area known as a barrio called Sal Si Puedes, Spanish for "Get Out If You Can." Rows of dilapidated

This is a general view of a makeshift tent dwelling built on wooden platforms in a camp for Dust Bowl migrants near Marysville, California. (Courtesy of the Associated Press)

shacks and rundown houses lined the two unpaved dead end streets running through the barrio.

For the newly arrived Chavezes, the problem was not getting out of the barrio; it was getting in. Juana asked around and learned there might be a room available. By that time, eleven members of the family were traveling in two cars. They crowded themselves into a ten by twelve-foot room in a boardinghouse. "The boys slept on one side, the girls on the other," Cesar recalled. "We even kept our belongings there, but we didn't have a choice. At most we had five dollars left."

Originally, the cherry farmers offered workers two cents a pound for picking their crop but because there were so many migrant workers seeking jobs, they lowered it to one-and-a-half cents. Once again, the Chavezes had no choice but to accept the wages offered.

For two weeks, they toiled in the cherry orchards. The little money they made went for food, gas, and rent.

The first job the Chavez family found in San Jose was picking cherries.

Once, Cesar's brother, Richard, stood out in the streets of the barrio and yelled: "We don't have food! We're poor!" Richard's pleas only earned him a scolding from Juana, who told him: "If you don't have any food, you keep your mouth shut. You don't say anything."

After the cherry harvest ended, the Chavezes went to work cutting and pitting apricots. The work was steadier than cherry picking, but was still tedious and low paying. The packinghouse allowed families to work together. Librado would go to the packing house at 5:30 AM and reserve spaces at a table for his family.

Many migrant families did not earn enough to pay for housing and had to survive in makeshift camps. (Courtesy of Walter P. Reuther Library, Wayne State University)

Because the Chavezes were inexperienced at cutting and pitting, they could not work as quickly as the other laborers. Working together, they made about thirty cents a day and ate apricots to keep from going hungry. When the apricot harvest ended, they were out of work again but could not afford to leave the barrio. They waited for another harvest while their funds dwindled away. They were able to hold out until the prune harvest, which gave them four weeks of steady work and decent housing. They earned twenty to thirty dollars a week while living in what seemed like a palace compared to the small cramped room in Sal Si Puedes. It had two bedrooms, electricity, and hot water. Cesar called the house and the prune harvest: "probably the best we ever lived." Wages from the prune harvest allowed them to buy items such as meat and school clothes. It was their first taste of the financial stability since leaving Arizona.

It didn't last long. After the prune harvest, they went to Oxnard, California to harvest walnuts. Cesar later called this "one of the worst winters in our lives." Men—not machines—were used to shake the walnuts loose. Librado used a long metal pole with a hook on the end to shake the tree limbs. He had to use all his might and muscle to strip a tree bare. Then, he would take a short break while the others picked up the walnuts.

When the walnut harvest ended, they were once again unemployed and homeless. Another migrant worker let them pitch a tent in a field behind her house. Although Oxnard was in southern California, the winters were damp and cold. When the fog rolled in off of the Pacific Ocean, the cold damp air left layers of dew. The dampness moistened the clothes and everything else left outside. Nothing would dry out completely. Librado dug a dike around the tent to keep out the rainwater. The tent was not large enough for the whole family and Cesar, Richard, and their cousin, Lenny, slept outside. They rigged up a bed with a piece of canvas over it to keep out the rain. "There, in the middle of nothing, we slept in that field, just between the dirt and the sky," said Cesar.

The persistent dampness eventually disintegrated Cesar's only pair of shoes. He had to walk to school barefooted. Cesar was teased unmercifully: "Going to school without shoes was an ordeal," he said. "Kids can be devastating and they never let me forget it."

Cesar's sister, Rita, was not able to endure the teasing and stopped going to school. Cesar stayed in school, but he was never able to get much formal education. He attended more than thirty different elementary schools but never went beyond the eighth grade. He dropped out after Librado was injured in an automobile accident in 1942.

Cesar's life became a succession of low paying, backbreaking farm jobs. Sometimes, he found work through friends who told him where the next harvest was. Most of the time, however, he had to find work by dealing with dishonest labor contractors that lured unsuspecting workers by promising more than they could deliver. They lied about the wages and living conditions and cheated them by claiming they had worked fewer hours than they actually had. When a worker complained, the contractor would call it an honest mistake and say that he did not have the money with him to make up the difference. Cesar later told an interviewer:

> It's not so much the money, it's the whole principle of being cheated out of something that you had to sweat so hard to earn. It's not like stealing fifteen cents from you, it's like somebody stealing fifteen cents of hard labor, which is an entirely different thing. It's a matter of destroying your manhood, taking away all your dignity.

The constant exploitation by farmers and labor contractors led Librado to join a union in hopes of achieving better pay and improved working conditions. This was Cesar's first introduction to organized labor.

The Congress of Industrial Organizations in Washington, D.C. (Library of Congress)

About 1939, we were living in San Jose. One of the old CIO (Congress of Industrial Organizations) unions began organizing workers in the dried-fruit industry, so my father and uncle became members. Sometimes the men would meet at our house and I remember seeing their picket signs and hearing them talk. They had a strike and my father and uncle picketed at night. It made a deep impression on me. But of course they lost the strike, and that was the end of the union. But from that time on, my father joined every new agricultural union that came along.

The failure of the union was disappointing, but it did not deter Cesar from wanting better pay and improved working conditions. The setbacks suffered by his father and uncle in their organizing activities increased Cesar's resolve to make a difference in the lives of his fellow migrant farmworkers.

Before Cesar could embark upon a life as a union and social activist, World War II intervened. Both of his parents, especially his pacifist mother, did not want Cesar to enlist. But when he turned seventeen, he knew he only had two options: enlist or wait to be drafted when he turned eighteen. "I don't know why I joined the Navy in 1944," Cesar said later. "I think mostly to get away from the farm labor. I was doing sugar beet thinning, the worst kind of backbreaking job, and I remember telling my father, 'Dad I've had it!'"

Cesar was miserable during his two years in the Navy. He resented the officers who assigned him menial work

Chavez served in the navy during World War II aboard a troop transport similar to this restored ship. (US Navy)

as a deckhand on a troop transport. Before World War II, the Navy had accepted racial minorities such as Filipinos and African Americans, but few Mexicans. During the war, the kitchen and food service jobs went to the Filipinos and African Americans, while nearly all of the Mexican sailors were deckhands.

Cesar discovered that discrimination was not limited to people with dark skin. He was surprised to find that white people would discriminate among themselves.

"I saw this white kid fighting because someone called him a Polack and I found out that he was Polish and hated the word Polack."

Cesar said. "He fought every time he heard it. I began to learn something; [I saw] that others suffered, too."

Cesar was most marked by an instance of discrimination that occurred when he was off duty. He was on a three-day leave and went to a movie theater in Delano, California. Like many other states at that time, California had segregated seating in movie theaters. Darker skinned people—Mexicans, Filipinos, and African Americans—were confined to a small section of seats in the right rear part of the theater. The rest of the seats were reserved for whites and Japanese.

Cesar deliberately sat in the section reserved for whites and Japanese. He was in his civilian clothes. If he had been dressed in his uniform, the theater management might have ignored his defiance:

> This time something told me that I shouldn't accept such discrimination. It wasn't a question of sitting elsewhere because it was more comfortable. It was just a question that I wanted a free choice of where I wanted to be. I decided to challenge the rule, even though I was very frightened.

When he was asked to move to the segregated section, Cesar refused. The police came and took him to jail, but they did not know how to charge him. The desk sergeant finally decided he could not charge Cesar with being drunk or disturbing the peace. Instead, he gave Cesar a lecture, and then released him after about a hour:

> He (the desk sergeant) tried to scare me about putting me in jail for life, the typical intimidation that they use. I was angry at what happened, but I didn't know how to proceed. It was the first time I had challenged rules so brazenly, but in our own way my family had been challenging the growers for some time. That was part of life.

In 1946, Cesar received an honorable discharge from the Navy. He returned to Delano and resumed working as a migrant farmworker. He also resumed his courtship of Helen Fabela, whom he had first met at a malt shop in Delano when he was sixteen and she was fifteen. Helen was in high school, but like Cesar, she had to drop out to help her family. Her father had died when she was only eleven. She began working in a grocery store, and Cesar became a regular customer.

Cesar and Helen were married in 1948. After their wedding, he used the family car to go on a two-week honeymoon touring Spanish missions in California. It was the longest vacation of his life.

Their first home was a one-room shack in a migrant workers' camp. It had no electricity or running water and a small kerosene camping stove provided inadequate protection against the bitter cold. They did not have a car, so Cesar was constantly asking friends for rides to and from work.

Hoping for a better life, Cesar borrowed some money to move to San Jose. Cesar's brother, Richard, and his parents were already living there. Richard had a steady job on an apricot farm. Cesar worked on the farm with Richard once or twice a week when extra help was needed. The rest of the time, he looked for work. Cesar's budget was strained even tighter after Fernando, the first of his eight children, was born. He, along with his parents, finally found steady work as sharecroppers on a strawberry farm outside of San Jose. In the sharecropping system, a tenant farmer raises the crop and then shares it with the landowner instead of paying rent.

Sharecropping gave Cesar and Helen a place to live with water and electricity and a twenty-five-dollar-a-week stipend for groceries and other expenses. In return, they worked long hours planting and picking the seven-and-a-half-acre strawberry crop. Despite all their hard work, they never made any money beyond the weekly twenty-five dollars for expenses. "For nearly two years we worked hard there without missing a day, not even Christmas," said Cesar. "Finally I left and made my dad break the agreement. We were really being taken. We hadn't made a dime."

At a local employment office Cesar learned that a lumber company in Crescent City, California, was recruiting workers. Crescent City was about four hundred miles north of San Jose. Cesar and Richard packed up their belongings and moved their families. The work was steady, but Helen never adjusted to the living conditions.

Very young children from migrant families were often put to work picking strawberries and other crops. (Courtesy of Walter P. Reuther Library, Wayne State University)

By that time Cesar and Helen had two children, and Helen was pregnant with a third child.

The strain of another pregnancy and the unrelenting northern California wind and rain was more than she could bear. After eighteen months, Richard, Cesar, and their families returned to San Jose where Cesar found work at a lumber mill and Richard got a job as a carpenter. They had escaped the fields but were not able to forget about the ones who were not so fortunate. Then Cesar and Richard met a Catholic priest and encountered a professor-turned-community-activist that would change the course of their lives.

CHAPTER 4.
An Activist's Beginnings

When Father Donald McDonnell became a priest in the Catholic Church he asked the Archdiocese of San Francisco to assign him to work and live in the San Jose barrio of Sal Si Puedes. He was committed to improving the lives of the migrant workers, many of whom were Catholics from Mexico.

After settling in Sal Si Puedes, McDonnell began walking the streets and sidewalks of the barrio. He would meet and greet the inhabitants and ask them to help him open a church in their neighborhood. He soon met Cesar Chavez, who enthusiastically supported his work. Chavez had never abandoned his devout Catholic faith and he began to accompany McDonnell and assist him when he performed mass at migrant labor camps.

As they spent time together McDonnell and Chavez discussed spiritual matters and also had long talks about the plight of farmworkers. McDonnell taught Chavez the history of the farmworkers' struggles and that fighting injustice and helping the less fortunate was a natural extension of their Catholic faith. Chavez remembered later that:

> He told me about social justice, and the Church's stand on farm labor and reading from the encyclicals of Pope Leo XIII, in which he upheld labor unions. I would do anything to get the Father to tell more about labor history. I began going to the bracero camps with him to help with the mass, to the city jail with him to talk to the prisoners, anything to be with him.

St. Francis of Assisi, who gave away all his property and founded the Franciscan order of monks in the twelfth century, was a spiritual inspiration to the Community Service Organization. (Library of Congress)

Eugene V. Debs (left) *organized one of the first industrial unions, the American Railroad Union. John L. Lewis* (right) *helped to found the Congress of Industrial Organizations, an umbrella group of several industrial labor unions.* (Library of Congress)

McDonnell also introduced Chavez to books that had not been available to him during his limited formal education. Chavez read the teachings of Saint Paul and about Saint Francis of Assisi, who founded a Catholic order dedicated to the ideal of absolute poverty for its preaching brothers. He also read about the American labor leaders, Eugene V. Debs and John L. Lewis.

The books that had the deepest influence on Chavez, though, were the writings of and biographies about Mahatma Gandhi, who had freed India from British rule through the use of nonviolent civil disobedience. The idea that lasting change could be achieved by nonviolent means intrigued Chavez. "I've been greatly influenced by Gandhi's philosophy and have read a great deal about what he said and did. But in those days I knew very little about him except what I read in the papers and saw in newsreels."

Gandhi was an inspiration, but it was Fred Ross who taught him how to be an effective organizer. Ironically, when Ross first tried to see Chavez, he was repeatedly turned away.

Mahatma Gandhi lead the fight to free his native India from British rule by the use of nonviolent civil disobedience, a technique later adopted by Martin Luther King Jr. and Cesar Chavez. (Library of Congress)

Saul Alinsky, founder of the Community Service Organization. (Library of Congress)

Fred Ross worked for the Community Service Organization (CSO), which was founded by a social activist named Saul Alinsky. While working as a criminologist, Alinsky had formed a firm belief that government was not effectively attacking the causes of crime:

> All the experts agreed the major causes of crime were poor housing, discrimination, economic insecurity, unemployment and disease. So what did we do for our kids? Camping trips and something mysterious called 'character building.' We tackled everything but the issues.

Alinsky first put his ideas into practice by working to transform a Chicago slum known as Back of the Yards because it was located behind the Chicago Stockyards. With the backing of local church and labor leaders, Alinsky led the residents in picketing, boycotts, rent strikes, and sit-down strikes that pressured local businesses, landlords, and politicians to make concessions. With Alinsky's help, the neighborhood transformed itself into a model working-lass community.

In 1946, Alinsky hired Ross to start an organization to help Mexicans and Latinos improve their living conditions.

Saul Alinsky began his work by trying to reform the neighborhoods around the Chicago Stockyards. (Library of Congress)

When that organization, which became the CSO, began organizing a chapter in Sal Si Puedes in 1952, Father McDonnell recommended Chavez to Ross as a potential recruiter and organizer.

One afternoon, Ross made an unexpected visit to Chavez's home. Helen answered the door and told Ross that Cesar was not at home. Ross politely thanked her and told Helen that he would try to see him some other time. When Cesar got home from work, Helen told him that some tall, lean white man had been by to see him. Chavez quickly decided that he did not want to have anything to do with him:

> We never heard anything from whites unless it was the police, or some sociologist from Stanford, San Jose State or Berkeley coming to write about Sal Si Puedes.

Fred Ross, here with Chavez, was hired as a young man by Saul Alinsky to form the Community Service Organization. (Courtesy of Walter P. Reuther Library, Wayne State University)

They'd ask all kinds of silly questions, like how did we eat our beans and tortillas. We felt that it wasn't any of their business how we lived.

Ross kept returning and Chavez kept avoiding him, usually by slipping away to Richard's house. Finally, Helen got tired of lying and making excuses for Cesar and told Ross where Richard lived. When they finally met, Ross told Chavez about the CSO, and he asked him to host an organizational meeting. Ross impressed Chavez with his earnest manner and fluent Spanish and he agreed to host the meeting. But he still had some suspicions about Ross and came up with a plan to sabotage the meeting.

I already had a plan in mind. I invited some of the rougher guys I knew and bought some beer. I thought that we could show this gringo a little bit of how we felt. We'd let him speak a while, and when I gave them a signal, shifting my cigarette from my right hand to my left, we'd tell him off and run him out of the house. Then we'd be even.

Chavez never put his plan into action. Before he could give the signal Ross won them over by speaking knowledgeably about the problems they faced in Sal Si Puedes. He talked about the creek in the barrio that was polluted by waste from a nearby packinghouse. He spoke compassionately about how their children were getting sores on their legs and feet from playing in the dirty water. Ross mentioned that the creek was a breeding ground for mosquitoes and attacked the local politicians for their apathy.

Ross also spoke about a notorious recent case in which five Los Angeles policemen were jailed for brutality after they had beaten up some Mexican prisoners. He reminded his rapt audience that the policemen were jailed because the CSO got involved in the case. As Ross spoke, Chavez lost his skepticism and began to believe that change was possible. "Fred did such a good job of explaining how poor people could build power that I could even taste it," Chavez said. "I could really feel it. I thought, gee, it's like digging a hole. There's nothing complicated about it."

After the meeting, when Chavez walked him to his car, Ross asked him if he would like to go to another meeting and Cesar accepted his invitation. Ross thought Chavez had the determination and perseverance to make a real commitment to the CSO:

> At the very first meeting, I was very much impressed with Cesar. I could tell that he was intensely interested, a kind of burning interest rather than one of those inflammatory things that lasts one night and is then forgotten. He asked many questions, part of it to see if I really knew, putting me to the test. But it was much more than that.

Ross was so sure of Chavez's commitment and natural abilities that he made a prophetic entry in his diary after their first meeting. "I kept a diary in those days. And the first night that I met Cesar, I wrote in it, 'I think I've found the guy that I'm looking for.' It was obvious even then."

A Community Service Organization voting registration center in 1958. (Courtesy of Walter P. Reuther Library, Wayne State University)

The first assignment Ross gave Chavez was to help with a voter registration drive for the 1952 elections. There would be primary elections in June followed by general elections in November. After working all day at the lumberyard, Chavez worked all evening registering new voters. He soon discovered that the local authorities had put many obstacles in his way: "There were restrictions on everything," Chavez said. "We couldn't speak Spanish when he were registering; we couldn't go door to door; we couldn't register except in daylight hours; we couldn't register on Sundays."

Chavez encountered further difficulties when he tried to recruit some friends to serve as deputy registrars. He recruited sixteen friends to fill the positions, but none of them had the necessary qualifications. Some could read

Spanish well, but not English. Others could read English, but not Spanish. A few others were ineligible because they had been convicted of felonies.

Despite the setbacks, Chavez refused to quit or even act discouraged. If his friends could not be registrars, they could still help him canvass Sal Si Puedes. By election day, Chavez and his friends had registered approximately six thousand new voters in an eighty-five-day drive.

The increase of Mexican and Latino voter registrations worried members of the local Republican Central Committee. They knew that these new voters would tend to vote for Democrats. The Republicans resorted to tactics of intimidation:

> We had registered so many that the Republican Central Committee decided to intimidate the people that were voting for the first time. Republicans at the polls challenged voters. 'Are you a citizen? Read from here!' People were scared away. Fred came to help us, and we tried unsuccessfully to get people to go back and vote. It was a disaster.

Following the election, the CSO board had an emergency meeting to decide how to respond to the intimidation tactics. Ross suggested sending a telegram to J. Howard McGrath, the United States attorney general. The telegram formally protested the harassment by the Republicans and asked for a formal investigation by the United States Department of Justice.

When Ross asked for someone on the CSO board to sign it, no one volunteered. Chavez was shocked: "I remember getting very upset. I didn't say anything, but inside of me I lost all respect for them."

A 1954 photo of the founders of the Community Service Organization. Cesar Chavez is second from right in the front; Fred Ross is sixth from right. Helen Chavez is third from the right in the back row. (Courtesy of Walter P. Reuther Library, Wayne State University)

Since no one else volunteered, Chavez raised his hand and told the board he would sign it. The Republicans responded to the charges by accusing Chavez and the CSO of registering illegal aliens and dead people. Chavez and the board responded by accusing the Republicans of bigotry.

The resulting publicity put Chavez's name in the paper and in the public spotlight. A short while later, FBI agents came to the lumberyard to interview him. "I was scared," said Chavez. "What had I done? I knew that I had never done anything wrong, but who knows."

The early 1950s were the years of the Red Scare, a period of hysteria over the fear that Communist spies were infiltrating United States institutions such

U.S. senator Joseph McCarthy accused many Americans of being secret Communists during the 1950s. (Library of Congress)

as entertainment, journalism, labor unions, and even the government itself. This scare was heightened by a U.S. senator from Wisconsin named Joseph R. McCarthy who used his powerful committee in the senate to accuse hundreds of public officials of being Communists or Communist sympathizers.

This fear of communism, and of being labeled "soft" on communism, spurred attacks against labor and civil rights organizations. Not surprisingly, the FBI agents tried to connect Chavez with Communism: "The agents starting asking me a lot of questions about Communism. I said, 'You know damn well I'm not a Communist!'"

After he had convinced the agents of his loyalty, they took Chavez to meet some members of the Republican Central Committee. The meeting quickly turned into a shouting match. Chavez was pleased, however, to hear the agents tell the Republicans that they could not intimidate voters.

After the voter registration drive, Chavez's next challenge was to establish a CSO chapter in Oxnard, a small town north of Los Angeles. The CSO had been invited into the Oxnard by the Packinghouse Workers Union (PWU), which had been trying to organize the migrant workers who worked in the packing sheds where produce was readied for shipment.

Although the union had won several elections to represent the packinghouse workers, it had been unable to get contracts from the employers. Members were discouraged, and the union was losing its membership. Chavez met with the migrant workers in Oxnard and asked them about their major complaints and concerns. What bothered the migrant workers the most was the continuing use of the bracero program, which reduced the number of jobs available to them and kept wages low.

During the war thousands of male workers were drafted into the armed forces. Women and men who were too old to serve found better paying jobs working in factories making munitions, ships, aircraft, and other items vital to the war effort, and the federal government allowed farmers to hire Mexican nationals to harvest certain crops. When World War II ended there were an estimated fifty thousand Mexican citizens, or braceros, working in America. The bracero program was supposed to end after the war, but politically influential growers and farmers convinced Congress there was still a shortage of workers and Congress extended the bracero program. By 1953, there were an estimated two hundred thousand braceros working in the fields. By law, braceros could only be used when other workers were not available, but labor department officials routinely ignored the law.

Chavez learned how the system worked when he went to a bracero camp and applied for work. He was told to go the Farm Placement Service in Ventura, about eight miles outside of Oxnard. The hiring office in Ventura did not open until 8:00 AM, two hours after the workers at the bracero camp had been sent out on jobs.

The people at the hiring office gave Chavez a referral slip for employment. When Chavez showed the slip the next morning, he was told that it was outdated. If he did not have a slip with the current date on it he could not work. "That was the gimmick," said Chavez. "The whole system was rotten. The Farm Placement System (FPS) was in cahoots with the federal government, which was in cahoots with the growers to keep the local workers out of jobs, get all of the braceros in, and then exploit the braceros." Even when farmworkers got assignments from the FPS, the braceros were being used in their places.

From August 1958 to November 1959, Chavez worked to organize the farmworkers of Oxnard to fight the bracero program. He was able to document hundreds of cases of illegal employment discrimination by having unemployed farm-workers fill out daily work cards. He kept records of how they were passed over in favor of available bracero workers.

He also began to use some of the tactics he would later employ with the United Farm Workers (UFW). Chavez organized sit-ins during which unemployed farmworkers would go out into the fields and station themselves opposite the braceros. He also led protest marches that attracted the attention of the media. At the end of a march, the marchers burned their FPS-issued work cards as a symbolic protest. Chavez invited reporters to watch.

The resulting publicity eventually forced the growers to give in. Rather than asking publicly for workers, the growers began to call Chavez and tell him to send workers to a designated pickup area at a certain time. At other times, the growers came directly to the CSO office, which soon became a hiring hall.

In addition to getting increased wages and job opportunities for his followers, Chavez brought about some changes in the FPS. The director was fired for taking bribes, and lost his pension. Several other corrupt FPS employees were fired.

Chavez had been successful but he was afraid it would not last. "We had won a victory, but I didn't realize how short-lived it would be," said Chavez later. "We could have built a union there, but the CSO wouldn't approve. . . . I wanted to go for a strike and get some contracts, but the CSO wouldn't let me." He was convinced that long-term success would only come from having a strong, permanent union of farmworkers.

At that time, all Chavez could do was go back to the CSO office and file a report. He could document the discrimination, but little would change. But Fred Ross had been right—Cesar Chavez was determined and persistent. He continued to immerse himself in his work with the CSO, while becoming increasingly convinced he could accomplish more by starting his own union.

CHAPTER 5.

The Black Eagle Takes Flight

At the 1962 national convention of the CSO Chavez proposed that they should create a union just for farmworkers but the members voted it down. Chavez's first reaction after the vote was to form the union himself, but he allowed himself to be talked out of it. "I thought of doing it alone," Chavez said, "but I was discouraged by some friends, mostly some of the priests that I worked with."

Chavez's friends were convinced that the union could succeed only with the backing of the powerful AFL-CIO, which was made up of the two most powerful unions in the country. The AFL (American Federation of Labor) was founded in 1886 to organize skilled workers into nation-wide unions to work for higher wages, shorter workdays, and safer and healthier working conditions. Most of their members worked in the building trades or as coal miners or railroad workers. The CIO (Congress of Industrial Organizations) was founded in 1935 to organize workers in such heavy industries as steel, automotive, and electrical, as well as workers in the textile, rubber,

George Meany was the longtime leader of the powerful AFL-CIO, an umbrella group of labor unions. (Library of Congress)

and garment industries. After competing against each other for members for twenty years, the organizations merged in 1955.

The AFL-CIO had to be pressured into supporting a farmworkers' union. Two Catholic priests, Father Thomas McCullough and Father Donald McDonnell, met with the AFL-CIO's top leaders, Walter Reuther and George Meany and told them about the deplorable conditions of California farmworkers, and to complain that the AFL-CIO was doing nothing to help them.

It took about a year for the AFL-CIO to make a commitment to help farmworkers. It finally established the Agricultural Workers Organizing Committee (AWOC) in

Father Thomas McCullough (center), *holding a religious service for migrant Mexican farm laborers in a work camp, supported the farmworkers union.* (Courtesy of Time Life Pictures/Getty Images.)

1959 and then sent a few professional organizers to help the farmworkers.

The AWOC was able to get pay raises for a few farmworkers, but had trouble recruiting members. Most of their organizers were white and had never done farm work. The Mexican and Hispanic farmworkers did not think the white organizers understood their needs.

The AWOC's efforts to organize farmworkers were also hampered by its chummy relationship with the labor contractors. AWOC organizers were instructed to work directly with the Mexican and Hispanic workers, but instead they

Current photo of Dolores Heurta, cofounder of the United Farm Workers union. (Courtesy of the Associated Press)

used the Spanish-speaking contractors as middlemen and to collect union dues. Most of the farmworkers saw the dues collections as just another form of exploitation. Although the workers received small pay raises, little else was done to improve their situation. It appeared to the workers that the AWOC was working with the contractors instead of looking out for their interests.

Dolores Huerta, who had worked with Chavez at the CSO, vainly tried to get the AWOC to hire him to train their union organizers. When they refused, Chavez convinced Huerta to leave the organization.

In 1960 the AWOC embarked on a long, bitter strike with the lettuce growers in California's Imperial Valley. The strike collapsed in 1961 because the AWOC and the union representing the packinghouse workers argued and were unable to present a united front. When the strike failed, the AFL-CIO withdrew its financial support from the AWOC.

While the AWOC and the packinghouse workers were bickering, Chavez wondered if he should remain with the CSO. He had been rebuffed every time he asked the leadership to support a union of farmworkers. Finally, he issued an ultimatum and told their board: "If CSO doesn't go for this farm labor project, I'm going to leave the organization."

Chavez thought he had won them over when the board said they would back his union. But when they voted on it at their national convention, it was voted down again. He now felt that he had no choice. During the national convention in March 1962, Chavez announced his resignation from the CSO.

Following his resignation, Chavez was offered a job paying two hundred dollars a week with the AWOC. He would be paid much more than he had been at his CSO job, but he turned it down. He sensed that the AFL-CIO was not going to keep supporting the AWOC. "I just knew that big organization wasn't going to let a little organization get it into trouble," said Chavez. "They had too many things at stake, if we started raising hell with strikes and boycotts. My only hope of success was if no strings were attached."

Chavez left the CSO on his thirty-fifth birthday. He packed up his car and took a rare vacation with his

Cesar and Helen Chavez with their six children in 1968. (Courtesy of Walter P. Reuther Library, Wayne State University)

family. They spent about a week in the beachfront town of Carpinteria. They could not afford a motel and pitched a tent on the beach. While his family played in the sand and surf, Chavez planned a new farmworkers' union. He decided that his first move would be to return to Delano because it was Helen's hometown. "I knew that no matter what happened, we would have a roof over our heads and a place to get a meal," Chavez said.

After settling in Delano, Chavez drew up a map of the eighty-six towns between Arvin and Stockton, California. He decided to visit each and talk to the farmworkers about forming a union. He visited both their work sites and the *colonias* (camps) in which the workers lived. When he asked them what they thought about forming a union, their responses were not encouraging. The most common reactions were fear or disbelief. Occasionally, some worker would say that it was a good idea, but only rarely did he get a strong positive response.

Chavez decided to change his tactics and to have small house meetings to talk about unionizing. The workers talked more freely when they were inside someone's home because they were less fearful of reprisal. "When I talked to people at their homes, it was unbelievable how their attitude changed, how different it was when I talked to them in the fields," said Chavez. "When they overcame their fear, almost all of them would agree that a union was a good thing." Still, Chavez found the workers' enthusiasm and approval were blunted by a sense of defeat. Most of the workers believed that the growers were too powerful.

Sixteen-hour days were the norm for Chavez when he was organizing and recruiting. When he was not holding meetings or talking to workers, he was dropping off questionnaires and mimeographed cards in grocery stores. The cards asked the workers how much they thought they should be paid.

While Chavez was out organizing and recruiting, Helen was doing what she could to support the family. During the grape harvest, she worked ten hours a day, five days a week for about eighty-five cents an hour.

Sundays were the only time that Chavez was not out organizing and meeting with workers, but this was not a day of rest. Instead, he worked digging ditches. He had had $1,200 in savings when he started organizing the union, but that money was going fast. Sometimes, he would ask the workers to provide food for his family. "It turned out to be about the best thing that I could have done," Chavez recalled. "Although at first it's hard on your pride. Some

Jose Martinez, Dolores Huerta, Tony Orendain, and Cesar Chavez at the founding convention of the National Farm Workers Association, September 1962. (Courtesy of Walter P. Reuther Library, Wayne State University)

of the best members came in that way. If people give you their food, they'll give you their hearts."

The donation of a mimeograph machine from a church was another valuable contribution to the fledgling union. Chavez set up the machine in his brother Richard's garage and began churning out flyers, cards, and questionnaires to recruit members.

Before the union even had a name, Chavez had become the man to see when a worker was cheated of his wages or suffered an accident on the job. He would pressure the grower. Sometimes it was a direct visit; at other times a friendly lawyer or a concerned priest would intervene.

The National Farm Workers Association flag was unveiled in 1962.

About six months after settling in Delano, Chavez decided that it was time for the union to have its first convention. On September 30, 1962, about 250 supporters met in an abandoned movie theater in Fresno for the first convention of the National Farm Workers Association (NFWA).

One of the highlights of the convention was the introduction of a flag. Chavez had initially wanted the flag to have an eagle similar to the one on the Mexican flag. His brother, Richard, sketched a design with an eagle holding a cluster of grapes in its claws. Chavez liked his brother's design, but he was concerned that it would be hard to reproduce. He then gathered several graphic artists to produce a new design with straight lines and corners. The new flag featured a large, black Aztec eagle on a white circle with a red background. "I chose the colors, red with a black eagle on a white circle. Red and black flags are used for strikes in Mexico. They mean a union," said Chavez. The white circle signified the aspirations and hopes of the NFWA, the black eagle symbolized the plight of the farmworkers, and the red stood for the sacrifices they would need to make.

When the flag was unveiled, there was a mixed reaction from the convention-goers. Chavez recalled that everyone gasped, and a few were even shocked. Some did not like the color scheme, and others worried that the color combination resembled the Nazi banner. But after Manuel Chavez, Cesar's cousin, explained the colors and symbolism, the convention-goers voted to adopt the flag. Then they moved on to other matters. They agreed to lobby the governor and legislature for a $1.50-an-hour minimum wage and unemployment benefits for California farmworkers, but shied away from calling themselves a union. They instead used the term "association," although their goals and objectives were the same as a union's. The NFWA advocated for the right of farmworkers to engage in collective bargaining with their employers. Chavez also introduced an ambitious agenda that included establishing a NFWA credit union and a hiring hall.

After the convention adjourned, Chavez finalized a constitution for the NFWA. Because so many farmworkers were transients, he knew it would be difficult to establish strong local chapters. "Because of the mobility of the people, I thought that we would need a very strong, centralized, administration, and that we could never have a local as other unions have," said Chavez. "We couldn't have any geographical restrictions on employment . . . But we also wanted local say-so for the workers."

Chavez formulated much of the union's constitution after reading and studying federal laws protecting the rights of workers. The union's constitution granted free speech to workers for example, and to protect workers who had been discriminated against, or terminated, for speaking out about their working conditions.

Early on the NFWA had more setbacks than victories, but Chavez refused to be discouraged. The monthly union dues were only $3.50, but members would routinely drop out when Chavez tried to collect them or apologetically tell him they did not have the money. Although Chavez did not take their actions personally, he worried constantly about whether the union would suceed:

> There were times of course, when we didn't know whether we'd survive. . . . We might go all day collecting dues and have every single one say, 'I can't pay. I'm sorry, but I don't want to belong anymore.' That happened often, they would come and use us, and after they had gotten what they wanted, they had second thoughts. At times it took a lot of faith and courage not to turn against those people.

Although he found dunning members for dues distasteful, Chavez knew that if the union could not support itself, it would lose its independence. "We had to do it [collect dues] because we didn't want any money from the outside world. That's the only way that a Union can be supported, by its members," said Chavez.

The NFWA started out with two hundred members who pledged to faithfully pay the monthly dues. Ninety days later, only a dozen members were making the payments, but membership increased steadily from that point. Using social gatherings such as dances, barbecues, speeches, and fiestas, the NFWA began to attract new members. Chavez found that if members would pay dues for six months, then they would stick with the union.

Within a year of founding the NFWA, Chavez was convinced that the union would last. He set a three-year timetable for making a real difference in the lives of its members.

> Before our first year was up, we knew that we were on the right road with the Union. I'm not saying that we had it made, but the hardest bridge had been crossed. We gave ourselves three years of hard work. If we couldn't do it in three years, then we couldn't do it.
>
> But we made a firm promise among ourselves that if we couldn't do it, we'd never blame the people, we'd blame ourselves.

CHAPTER 6.

The First Strike

In the spring of 1965 the NFWA called its first strike. It began when a Mexican immigrant named Epifanio Camacho decided to do something about working conditions in the rosebush industry. Camacho worked for Mount Arbor, a company that employed about eighty-five workers in its fields.

Camacho and the other workers in the rosebush industry performed labor that required speed and precision and required them to crawl for hours on their knees. The workers had to quickly cut up mature rosebushes and then insert buds onto the mature plants. If they made the slightest mistake or miscalculation, the buds would not bloom and the rosebush would be useless.

A worker in the California grape fields. (Library of Congress)

Despite the skilled nature of his labor, Camacho had long endured broken promises over his pay. He and the workers had been promised nine dollars for every thousand plants but were only getting between $6.50 and seven dollars. One of Camacho's friends told him "Go see Cesar Chavez who lives over in Delano. He wants to organize the farmworkers."

When they first met, Chavez told Camacho to organize his fellow workers for a discrete house meeting. They had to be careful because Camacho had a reputation for being a troublemaker and managers at Mount Arbor had warned the workers that anyone who teamed up with Camacho would be fired. Only four workers showed up for the first house meeting, but thirty were at the second meeting. Ultimately, they decided to call a strike against Mount Arbor, the largest rose growing company. Before striking, the workers agreed that would not set up picket lines to prevent replacement workers from taking over their jobs.

On the Sunday before the strike, the workers held a solemn ceremony. Dolores Huerta held up a crucifix and the workers placed their hands on it and vowed to stick together throughout the strike. In a letter to Fred Ross, Chavez wrote: "Things are getting exciting. The most exciting thing is our drive to get a contract this summer. . . . If we are successful, we will have something to crow about."

On the first morning of the strike, Chavez sent out cars to check on the workers. Five or six workers were already up and dressed for work when Chavez's helpers called on them. The workers were too embarrassed to sabotage the strike by going to work after receiving those visits.

When the workers failed to report to work, Mount Arbor retaliated by bringing in a crew from Tangansiguieros, Mexico. Chavez and his followers responded by sending a letter to the town's mayor that he posted on the town bulletin board. Word soon spread that the local workers had betrayed their countrymen by breaking a strike and taking their jobs.

After four days of trying to find enough replacement workers, Mount Arbor was desperate to bring back their experienced workers and agreed to raise the workers' salaries. The raise was a victory for Chavez and the NFWA, but Mount Arbor never did follow through on its promises. In addition, Camacho was blacklisted—prevented from ever working again—in the rose industry.

While the NFWA was winning salary concessions from Mount Arbor, a bigger strike was brewing. In 1963 California growers had imported 65,000 braceros to work

Chavez and California governor Pat Brown (above) *pressured President Lyndon Johnson to end the program allowing Mexican workers to come to California during harvesttimes.* (Library of Congress)

President Lyndon B. Johnson signed a bill allowing more workers to be imported to work the California farms. (National Archives)

in their fields. The growers feared that there would be a shortage of workers when the program ended and used their political clout to put pressure on California governor Pat Brown and President Lyndon B. Johnson. Instead of ending the program, President Johnson amended it to allow more braceros to come to the United States in the summer of 1965, but they had to be paid at least $1.40 an hour.

Most of the thousands of Mexicans who came to the United States as part of the bracero program were experienced farmworkers who came north to make more money than they could in Mexico. The growers took advantage of the braceros and their need for employment and had them sign contracts written in English that kept them from knowing about their rights as workers and the conditions of their employment. The braceros planted and harvested such crops as sugar beets, cucumbers, and tomatoes. By the 1960s an influx of illegal workers crossing the border and increased automation for harvesting cotton had greatly reduced the demand for bracero labor.

The continuation of the bracero program gave strength

Chavez agreed that the National Farm Workers would support the Filipino workers when they struck the grape vineyards near Delano, California. (Courtesy of Walter P. Reuther Library, Wayne State University)

and momentum to the NFWA. During California's grape harvest in the spring of 1965, growers in the Coachella Valley decided to pay their workers $1.25 an hour but the Filipino workers soon discovered that the braceros were making $1.40 an hour. The AWOC then called on the workers to strike but after only ten days. After ten days the growers raised wages, but the workers did not get a contract. When the grape harvest moved north, other growers refused to pay the standard bracero wage of $1.40 an hour to other migrant farmworkers. In the Delano area, the same growers who had agreed to pay $1.40 an hour in the Coachella Valley were only paying a dollar an hour to workers other than braceros.

In September of 1965 Chavez learned that Filipino workers in nine vineyards in the Delano area had gone on strike with the backing of the AWOC. Chavez had to decide if the NFWA was going to support them. He was reluctant because he did not think that the NFWA had the resources. At that time the NFWA had around 1200 members, but only about two hundred paid their dues regularly. The union had around seventy dollars in its treasury and no backing from the AFL-CIO. Chavez thought that the NFWA was about two years away from being powerful enough to go on strike against the growers. But he did see advantages:

> I thought the growers were powerful and arrogant, and I judged that they were going to underestimate us, but I wasn't afraid of them or their power. I was afraid of the weakness of the people. I knew that the only way

Larry Itliong was the leader of the Filipinos working in California's grape fields. (Courtesy of Walter P. Reuther Library, Wayne State University)

we could win was to keep fighting for a long time, and I didn't see how we could get that determination.

After meeting with the union board, Chavez decided that the NFWA would support the strikers. He believed publicity would be their strongest weapon. If they could make the world outside of Delano aware of their dilemma, the strike would succeed. Otherwise, the local police and courts would quash it.

The Filipino workers were led by Larry Itliong, who had worked in the fields for more than thirty-five years. Itliong sympathized with the workers, but was reluctant to lead a strike. He warned his fellow Filipino workers

Chavez was inspired by Martin Luther King Jr.'s leadership of the civil rights movement. (Library of Congress)

that there were plenty of Hispanic workers willing to take their jobs in the vineyards at just about any wage. Itliong warned them that things could get brutal. "We told them," Itliong said, "they're going to suffer a lot of hardship, maybe you're going to get hungry, maybe you're going to lose your car, maybe you're going to lose your house. They said, 'We don't care.'"

However, even though they wanted to go on strike, the Filipino workers did not want to picket their bosses. Itliong had to work out a compromise. He agreed to let the Filipino workers picket bosses other than their own.

The growers were confident that the workers would return to work in a few days. To their surprise, the strike spread. During its first week, nearly two thousand workers in twenty labor camps joined. The growers brought in strikebreakers, derisively called scabs by the union members, to replace the strikers. The growers also tried to force the striking workers out of the labor camps by shutting off the gas and electricity. At other camps, they used armed security guards to keep the striking workers out.

The strike occurred at a time when there were frequent demonstrations of civil disobedience in the United States. The civil rights movement was in full swing. Hundreds of black Americans marched and boycotted stores and businesses to protest legal discrimination. The U.S. involvement in the Vietnam War and the increasing death toll had begun to inspire an antiwar movement. This atmosphere of social protest made it an auspicious time to examine attitudes toward farmworkers.

Chavez set September 16, 1965, as the date of the NFWA vote on whether to support the strike. That date had a special significance for many NFWA members because September 16 was Mexican Independence Day.

Emiliano Zapata, a leader in the Mexican Revolution against Spain, was an inspirational figure to Chavez and other leaders of the National Farm Workers Association.

Chavez chose it to capitalize on the holiday's association with freedom.

An overflow crowd of more than 1,500 people poured into the parish hall at Our Lady of Guadalupe Church in Delano. Members hoisted a huge NFWA flag and posters of the Mexican revolutionary Emiliano Zapata. When Chavez spoke, he reminded the audience of Mexico's struggle to free itself from Spanish rule. "155 years ago in the state of Guanajuato, Mexico, a padre proclaimed the struggle for liberty," Chavez said. "He was killed, but ten years later Mexico won its independence."

Chavez then shifted from talking about the past to talking about the present. "We are engaged in another struggle for the freedom and dignity which poverty denies us," he said. "But it must not be a violent struggle even if violence is used against us. Violence can only hurt us and our cause."

Chavez concluded his remarks by urging the NFWA members to support the strike: "The strike was begun by the Filipinos, but it is not exclusively for them. Tonight, we must decide if we are to join our fellow workers in this great labor struggle."

Chavez followed his speech by having Epifanio Camacho and other farmworkers speak. Camacho exhorted the crowd to support the strike by reciting some slogans from the Mexican Revolution. "It's better to die on our feet than live on our knees," he shouted.

Another farmworker named Felipe Navarro spoke of how he had seen a rancher murder two striking workers in the

1930s. Navarro sadly recalled that nothing was ever done to bring the rancher to trial. He said: "There was nothing to eat in those days, there was nothing. And we're still in the same place today, still submerged, still drowned."

Other workers spoke of past injustices, of exploitation, and of deprivation. Cries of "Strike!" filled the parish hall. Then Chavez and the other NFWA leaders asked for a show of hands. According to Chavez, there was unanimous agreement to support the strike.

Following the vote, the workers signed cards saying that they wanted the NFWA to represent them during the strike and agreed the NFWA would make the same demands as the AWOC—$1.40 an hour plus an incentive rate of twenty-five cents for every basket of grapes they picked. A good worker could pick nearly four baskets in an hour. Finally, they agreed that the strike would be nonviolent.

Chavez still held some hope that a strike could be averted. He asked the NFWA members to wait until the following Monday, September 20, before striking. If a strike did occur, he wanted the public to know that the workers had tried to mediate the dispute.

Letters were sent to all of the growers asking them to meet with the labor leaders. All but one of them was returned unopened. The only opened letter had been addressed to a grower who had died. It became apparent to Chavez that the strike would begin that Monday. What was not apparent to him at the time was how long and bitter the strike would be, or that it would transform him from an obscure local labor leader into a nationally recognized figure.

CHAPTER 7.

"Viva La Causa"

In the predawn hours of September 20, 1965, Chavez and eighty other workers joined a caravan of cars headed for Delano's second-largest vineyard. Their destination was a 4,500-acre ranch owned and operated by Schenley Industries. When the sun lit up the eastern sky above the Sierra Nevada, strikers were stationed at all twenty entrances to the vineyard. As the strikebreakers drove to work, they heard the picketing workers yelling at them. "Strike! Don't work here! Don't betray your brothers! Think things through!"

A few strikebreakers turned around or joined the picketers. Most, however, sped into the vineyard. At one entrance a couple of Schenley foremen tried to intimidate the picketers by driving tractors at them. They drove to within a few feet of the strikers and used their steel plow disks to kick up big clouds of dust.

Numerous other incidents of growers harassing and intimidating strikers occurred. One angry grower pointed a shotgun at two picketers and threatened to kill them and set their picket signs on fire. Other picketers were assaulted. "The growers were giving us the knee and the elbow, knocking us down and throwing us down. But we remained nonviolent. We weren't afraid of them. We just got up and continued picketing."

Eventually the picketers became discouraged. When they asked Chavez what they were accomplishing by striking, he explained that the strike affected production:

> Just keep talking to the scabs. After a while, if it's done the right way, they begin to leave. Somebody else may take their place, or it looks like the job is filled, but it isn't really. There's a loss of time. The grower is getting people who are not experienced, who have never seen grapes in their lives. For the employer, that's loss of money.

In the early weeks the number and energy of the picketers that Chavez could command varied. On a good day, the picketers were able to convince the strikebreakers to walk off the job. On the worst days, they could not get any pickets out because they did not have any money for transportation.

Chavez began to speak at churches and colleges to ask for help. While making a speech at the University of California in Berkeley, he announced that forty-four picketers had been arrested that morning. What he said was true, but he had orchestrated the arrests before the speech.

A member of the National Farm Workers Association yelling "Huelga!" during the 1966 strike. (Courtesy of Walter P. Reuther Library, Wayne State University)

The pickets were arrested merely for yelling: "*Huelga! Huelga!*" (Strike! Strike!) at a crew of strikebreaking workers. Chavez's wife, Helen, was one of the picketers. He knew he had to create dramatic moments to win the support of those wealthy enough to provide it.

Chavez asked the Berkeley students to donate their lunch money. The same day he made similar appeals at

San Francisco State University, Mills College, and Stanford University. In one day, he raised around $6,700, mostly from small donations. In addition to the much needed money, the students donated food and clothing and some responded to Chavez's invitation to come to Delano to witness the activity. Soon California college students were joining the picketers.

No amount of money or additional picketers, however, could stop the harassment. Police were stationed at the union office and at the homes of Chavez and other union leaders around the clock to record the license numbers of anyone who visited them. The police tailed Chavez and those closest to him constantly. "Every time I got in the car in Delano, they'd follow me all over, and I wouldn't shake them until I was well past several towns," Chavez said.

Strikers were also subject to harassment on the picket lines. In the early weeks deputies began photographing and interviewing the strikers, holding up the formation of a picket line for an hour or more.

At first, Chavez had everyone respond with total cooperation. When that tactic was not successful, the picketers switched to total noncooperation:

> Finally, we made up our minds that we'd been harassed enough. We refused to give them any information or let them take our pictures. We told the inquiring officer from the Kern County Sheriff's office that if he wanted more information from us or wanted to take our picture, he would have to arrest us. And at that point, we were able to gain some ground.

The strike widened when they set up a picket line on the docks in San Francisco. Members of the International Longshoremen's and Warehousemen's Union (ILWU) refused to cross the picket line. This action prevented grapes that were picked by nonstriking workers from being loaded onto ships for export. Chavez knew stopping a few ships was not going to be enough and decided the strike should concentrate on stopping the sale of grapes in the United States.

By December, Chavez had narrowed the focus of the strike to Schenley Industries. They would attack the company by encouraging the public not to buy their products, a tactic known as an economic boycott. If the sales of Schenley products dropped significantly, then the company would lose money. If the losses continued, Schenley would be forced to settle the strike.

The NFWA sent organizers to major United States cities to set up boycotts. Their most publicized effort was in Boston where they organized a Boston Grape Party to emulate the Boston Tea Party held by colonial revolutionaries in 1773. Instead of tea, they dumped grapes into Boston Harbor.

The strike gained some additional momentum when United Auto Wokers (UAW) president, Walter Reuther, pledged that his union would give $5,000 a month to both the AWOC and the NFWA. He made the announcement during a speech at the Filipino Hall. Reuther lifted the spirits of the workers by declaring: "This is not your strike, it is our strike."

Walter Reuther, center, pledged that his union, the United Auto Workers, would support the National Farm Workers in 1966. Here Reuther is picketing with Larry Itliong (left) *and Chavez* (right). (Courtesy of Walter P. Reuther Library, Wayne State University)

Reuther also met with the mayor and city manager of Delano, as well as with the growers who had refused to meet with Chavez. He urged the growers to recognize the union and advised them: "Sooner or later, these guys are going to win." The growers rebuffed Reuther by insisting the NFWA did not represent the workers and that the workers were happy with their jobs.

Thanks to the infusion of funds, the strikers returned to the picket lines. As the strike continued, prominent politicians and members of the national news media came to Delano. In March 1966 the California State Senate's Subcommittee on Un-American Activities came to Delano to investigate the strike.

The same month, the United States Senate's

Senator Robert Kennedy came to California to support the 1966 march and strike.
(Courtesy of the Associated Press)

Subcom-mittee on MigratoryLabor came to Delano for a public hearing. Two of the subcommittee's most prominent members were California Republican Senator George Murphy and Robert F. Kennedy, a Democrat from New York. Murphy was a conservative who had a been a supporter of the growers, but Kennedy sympathized with the strikers. Since being elected to the Senate almost a year after his brother, President John F. Kennedy, was assassinated on November 22, 1963, Robert F. Kennedy had been touted as a potential presidential candidate in 1968. The escalation of U.S. involvement in the Vietnam War had made the incumbent president, Lyndon B. Johnson, more vulnerable to challengers from within his own party.

Chavez made Senator Murphy uncomfortable when he produced affidavits accusing growers of illegally bringing in strikebreaking workers from Mexico and other areas. Chavez noted that the imported workers were never told they would be working as strikebreakers. He also reminded the senators that Congress had failed to enact laws giving them the basic rights that workers in many other industries took for granted, such as a minimum wage, collective bargaining, and the abolition of child labor.

"All that these bills do is say that people who work on farms should have the same human rights as people who work in construction crews, or in factories, or in offices," Chavez declared. He concluded his testimony by comparing the workers in the vineyards to plantation slaves: "Ranchers in Delano say that farmworkers are happy living the way they are—just like the Southern plantation owner used to say about the Negroes."

The most confrontational exchange came when Senator Kennedy questioned Roy Galyen, the sheriff of Kern County, California. Kennedy had been disturbed by Chavez's testimony that the sheriff had ordered his deputies to interrogate and take photos of all of the picketers. The New York senator was also bothered by the news of mass arrests of picketers by the sheriff's department. He asked Galyen if he took pictures of everyone in Delano. Galyen replied: "Well, if he is on strike, or something like that."

Kennedy then asked Galyen why the picketers were being arrested and he responded that it was his duty to arrest the picketers if he believed that a riot or some sort of major disturbance was about to erupt. Kennedy followed up by asking Galyen who had told him that there was going to be a riot. "The men right out there in the field that they were talking to said that if you don't get them out of here we're going to cut their hearts out," Galyen responded.

That response caused Kennedy to ask Galyen how he could arrest people when they had not broken any law. Galyen's answered that he was being proactive because the people he arrested were ready to break the law. Kennedy was not swayed by Galyen's logic and told the sheriff that he needed to read the Constitution of the United States.

After the televised hearings ended, Chavez decided to do something else to keep the strike in the national news. Other NFWA members had approached Chavez with the idea of going on a long march to publicize the continuing strike. An early idea was to march from California to Schenley's national headquarters in New York. Another proposal was to stage a march to Mexico to protest the recruitment of strikebreakers.

Ultimately Chavez and the other organizers decided to march from Delano to Sacramento, the state capital. After two days of planning, Chavez agreed that they would stage a twenty-five-day march that would end on Easter Sunday. The planners had three goals in mind—to call attention to the strike, to present their case to California

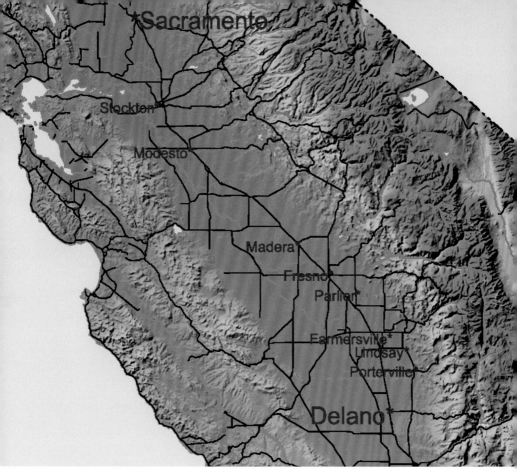

The three-hundred-mile march from Delano to Sacramento began on March 17, 1966.

governor Pat Brown, and to spread the strike to workers outside of the Delano area.

On March 17, 1966, Chavez and the striking farm-workers began the three-hundred-mile march from Delano to Sacramento. It would be the longest protest march in United States history.

The marchers were immediately confronted by the Delano police. They had planned to march north on Main Street in Delano, but a cordon of police officers stopped them by locking arms and forming a human chain to block their path. Chavez led the marchers to the edge of the police line where he told them: "We'll stay here if it takes a year, but we're going to march right through your city."

Fortunately for the marchers, there were still many members of the national news media in Delano. When they learned of the impasse there were soon photographers shooting pictures and reporters writing and broadcasting stories. After nearly three hours, the police relented and allowed the marchers to proceed.

The marchers formed a colorful procession. At the front of the march, standard bearers carried the flags of the United States, Mexico, and the Philippines. Many wore hats with red bands and the NFWA's black eagle. Others carried flags with the black eagle or the word *huelga* (strike). They also carried religious symbols, such as large crosses, Jewish stars of David, and portraits of the Virgin of Guadalupe, the matron saint of Mexico.

A team of FBI informants shadowed the marchers as they left Delano. One FBI agent sent a report to the agency's Washington headquarters: "March group began with about one hundred persons, about 75 percent Mexican Americans or Filipinos, and remainder Anglo Americans except for two or three Negroes," he wrote. "Affair was given publicity by all news media and will probably receive nationwide attention."

Along the way some marchers dropped out, but others took their place. Sometimes the line of marchers stretched two miles. When the marchers entered a new city or town along the route, supporters would be waiting to house and feed them.

Louis Valdez (center) *performing with El Teatro Campesino, a theater group organized to educate and inspire the workers during the 1966 strike.* (Courtesy of Walter P. Reuther Library, Wayne State University)

Every evening, the marchers presented a program to solicit support for the strike. They passed out copies of the Schenley boycott pledge and asked people to sign it and mail it to the corporation's vice-president. The pledge simply said that the signer would not purchase any Schenley products as long as the strike continued. They would finish with a round of songs and speeches.

One of the most inspiring parts of the nightly program was a young actor named Louis Valdez, who read an essay entitled "El Plan de Delano." (Valdez would go on to produce and direct such notable films as

Zoot Suit and *La Bamba*.) He would exhort his listeners by proclaiming:

> We are the sons of the Mexican Revolution. Along this road in the very same valley, the Mexican race has sacrificed itself for the last hundred years. Our sweat and our blood have fallen on this land to make other men rich. . . . We seek our basic, God-given rights as human beings. . . . We do not want the paternalism of the ranchers; we do not want the contractor; we do not want charity at the price of our dignity. We want to be equal with all the working men in the nation. Wherever

Chavez, limping from his blistered feet and swollen ankle, leading the march to the California capital in 1966. (Courtesy of Wayne State University)

there are Mexican people, wherever there are farmworkers, our movement is spreading like flames across
a dry plain. . . . Viva La Causa!

After nine days of marching, Chavez and his followers
entered the city of Fresno. By this time Chavez was in
great pain because he had not been wearing proper foot-
wear. Instead of wearing boots, he had been marching in a
pair of well-worn, low-cut shoes and had bleeding blisters
on his left foot, and his left leg was badly swollen from
the ankle to the thigh. He refused to take any painkillers
and after seven days of marching was also suffering from
a fever. He finally agreed to ride in a station wagon for
about an hour. After that he used a cane.

The reception that Chavez and the marchers received in
Fresno made him forget his agony. He would later remember
the warm welcome in Fresno as a turning point. Instead of
being harassed by the police, Fresno's mayor, Floyd Hyde,
assigned officers to run errands for the marchers:

> The march had really caught on by the time we got
> to Fresno. We had hundreds, if not thousands, of
> people marching in the city, mostly nonworkers,
> Fresno Chicanos. And the city gave us a royal welcome
> . . . . We had a rally at the Mexican theater, which was
> jam-packed. From then on, we were in good shape. It
> got bigger and bigger.

California governor Pat Brown had become aware of
the publicity the march had generated. On March 25 he

Vice President Hubert H. Humphrey supported the 1966 strike. (Library of Congress)

publicly announced that he would not be in Sacramento to greet the marchers when they arrived there on Easter Sunday but would be vacationing in Palm Springs that weekend. He ignored a telegram from the marchers asking him to meet with them in Palm Springs.

When the marchers arrived in Stockton, a crowd of nearly five thousand supporters greeted them. The strike was gaining national support as well. Chavez had been actively courting civil rights groups, liberal clergy, and progressive magazines. Soon other national political figures joined Senator Kennedy in his support of the strikers. Vice President Hubert H.

Humphrey and Minnesota senator Eugene McCarthy both lent their support to the strikers.

Shortly before the rally in Stockton, Gilbert Padilla approached Chavez and told him a representative of Schenley was on the phone waiting to discuss settling the strike. "The guy said that he wants to talk to you because he wants to sign a contract," Padilla said. "He says he's from Schenley."

Chavez reacted with disbelief. He assumed it was some kind of prank. He refused to take the call. "Oh, the hell with him!" Chavez said. "I've heard that story before."

Five minutes later, the Schenley representative called back. Padilla was more insistent this time. He told Chavez: "Cesar, he's got to talk to you!"

According to one source, a rumor that there would be a boycott of Schenley's liquor products by the California local of the International Bartenders Union forced the company to settle. When a union secretary had circulated a phony memo hinting at a boycott of Schenley's liquors the chairman of the board first reaction was to sell the company's five thousand acres of grapes. The company's lawyer talked him out of it and advised him to settle the strike and end the boycott instead.

Chavez traveled to Beverly Hills to meet with three important people—Schenley's lawyer, Sidney Korshak; Bill Kircher, the AFL-CIO's national organizing director; and a representative from the Teamsters Union. The negotiations came to a brief impasse when an AFL-CIO representative tried to talk Chavez into turning the NFWA over to the AWOC. Chavez quickly rebuffed the idea. "No!" he exclaimed. "You must be kidding. You're trying to tell me to give you a contract, when we fought for it, bled for it, and sweat for it. You must be out of your mind!"

A preliminary agreement was signed in a few hours. Schenley agreed to recognize the NFWA. The workers would get an immediate pay increase of thirty-five cents an hour. The agreement also paved the way for the NFWA to establish a credit union for its members.

National Farm Workers outside the state capitol building in Sacramento, California, Easter Sunday, 1966.
(Courtesy of Walter P. Reuther Library, Wayne State University)

On Easter Sunday 1966, Chavez and the other marchers entered Sacramento. A throng of around ten thousand people gathered on the steps of California's capitol building to wait for their arrival. It was raining, but the weather did not dampen the spirits of the marchers or their supporters. It was a time to celebrate. Chavez was elated by the agreement with Schenley, but he realized that it was only one company. The NFWA had won a battle, not a war. "It was an exciting end to our pilgrimage," said Chavez. "But we knew that it was only the end of the march. We still had an army of growers arrayed against us."

CHAPTER 8.

Army of Growers

The next company the NFWA locked horns with was the gigantic DiGiorgio Corporation, which had a reputation for being anti-union and for breaking strikes. In 1939, six hundred farmworkers went on strike at the company's orchards in Yuba City, California and DiGiorgio retaliated by getting the county government to pass a series of antipicketing laws. The retaliation did not end there. A sheriff's posse destroyed a soup kitchen that fed the strikers and forced them to leave the county, effectively ending the strike. DiGiorgio also used similar tactics to quell strikes in 1947 and 1960.

The NFWA pursued DiGiorgio after it summarily fired a worker named Adelina Gurola. Gurola was sorting plums when her supervisor dismissed her for taking a lunch break.

National Farm Workers picketing outside a produce terminal during the strike against the DiGiorgio Corporation. (Courtesy of Walter P. Reuther Library, Wayne State University)

During the break, she was approached by a young man passing out leaflets. Although Gurola was barely literate, she accepted the leaflet and stuffed it into her purse. When she returned to work, her supervisor brusquely told her: "Adelina, I don't got no place for you anymore."

Gurola was shocked and told her supervisor she had done nothing wrong and reminded him of her years of loyal service to the company. But she was fired with no chance of appeal or reinstatement. Later that day, a coworker came to Gurola's home and told her she had been fired for taking the leaflet. Only then did Gurola open her purse and look at the leaflet. She could read well enough to see that it had a return address in Bakersfield and that it asked farmworkers to join the NFWA. Angry, she got her boyfriend to drive her to Bakersfield.

When they arrived, they were surprised to see many other DiGiorgio employees waiting to enter the union's office. Gurola was hesitant to enter the office, but she decided she had nothing to lose.

Shortly after Schenley settled with the NFWA, the DiGiorgio management hinted it was willing to allow workers to vote to join a union. However, the company was not legally required to allow the workers to vote. Chavez was eager to negotiate with them, and traveled to Fresno to meet with company officials, but he abruptly called off the talks after receiving news that DiGiorgio employees were beating NFWA members. Some of DiGiorgio's guards had threatened a female union organizer at gunpoint and a male union member had been attacked and needed stitches to close his wound. Other union members were arrested, but DiGiorgio's guards were never charged with a crime. Chavez angrily told the company officials, "I'll be damned if I'm going to negotiate with you guys while you're beating and jailing our people!"

Chavez declared a boycott of DiGiorgio's products, and the NFWA and its supporters began to picket the company's corporate headquarters and the stores that carried DiGiorgio's products.

Seven months later both the boycott and the strike were faltering. Many of the union members were broke and the

NFWA did not have a large strike fund to support them. All the union could do was provide them with some food and supplies. The strikers were leaving the picket lines and returning to work.

Chavez needed to come up with a new strategy. In a series of secret meetings he urged the workers who had returned to DiGiorgio to be less productive and to work at a slower pace. He asked them to do "anything that was legal and moral, but that would cost the growers more money."

DiGiorgio fought this new strategy by importing migrant workers from Texas and Mexico. They were also able to get a court order restricting the number of pickets the union could use. The most disturbing news, however, was that they were requiring their new workers to sign cards authorizing the Teamsters Union to represent them.

Chavez opposed the Teamsters Union because of its history of corruption. In 1957, the Teamsters had been expelled from the AFL-CIO for corruption. That same year an investigation by a committee of the United States Senate linked the union with organized crime. Two presidents of the Teamsters Union, David Beck and Jimmy Hoffa, were imprisoned for bribery and attempted bribery and a third Teamsters president, Fred Fitzsimmons, died before he could begin his prison sentence.

In the meantime, negotiations continued with DiGiorgio. In June 1967 Chavez and Bill Kircher met with company officials. After several days of haggling, they agreed to take a short break, during which Chavez and Kircher learned that DiGiorgio had decided to hold elections at two of

Jimmy Hoffa, one-time leader of the Teamsters Union, was imprisoned for bribery and corruption. (Library of Congress)

their ranches. The news came as a complete surprise since DiGiorgio had not consulted with Chavez or Kircher.

The election ballots had four choices: the AWOC, the NFWA, the Teamsters or "no union." Instead of having a government arbitrator monitor the election, DiGiorgio planned to hire a public accounting firm. Kircher was so incensed at what he saw as an attempt to rig the election that he procured an injunction to have the names of the AWOC and the NFWA removed from the ballots. Chavez urged workers to boycott the vote and got his old friend Fred Ross to help to organize protests against the election.

On election day at DiGiorgio's Sierra Vista Ranch, Ross marshaled a crowd of about four hundred protesters across the street from the election hall. Chavez traveled to the other election site at DiGiorgio's Borrego Springs Ranch and led a group of picketers whom police had prevented from talking to the workers.

Chavez and the NFWA faced stiff competition from the Teamsters, who campaigned by calling Chavez a Communist and by providing free beer to workers willing to vote. Election officials helped the Teamsters by allowing DiGiorgio workers, such as stenographers and clerks, to vote, even though they were not farmworkers. The Teamsters won the election, but Chavez moved to get the results overturned.

The day after the election, Dolores Huerta attended the Mexican-American Political Association (MAPA) Convention in Fresno to ask the organization to put pressure on California governor Brown to call for a new election. Brown was running for re-election against actor-turned-politician Ronald Reagan and was seeking MAPA's endorsement. Reagan was the conservative, anti-union champion, which meant Brown would not get much support from company owners and managers. Although he had earlier avoided meeting with Chavez he agreed this time to ask DiGiorgio to hold a new election. Brown also appointed an independent arbitrator to rule on the validity of the election and asked DiGiorgio to delay negotiations with the Teamsters. The contested election had become national

Former actor Ronald Reagan defeated Pat Brown in 1966 to become governor of California. (Library of Congress)

news when Democratic senators Robert F. Kennedy and New Jersey's Harrison Williams asked DiGiorgio to hold off negotiations with the Teamsters. Brown appointed an arbitrator and asked the American Arbitration Association to investigate the election.

Chavez kept the pressure on DiGiorgio by going to the Borrego Springs Ranch to organize a strike. He was

Members of the National Farm Workers protested the arrest of Chavez in December 1971 with a march to the courthouse in Salinas. (Courtesy of Walter P. Reuther Library, Wayne State University)

arrested after he accompanied some striking workers back to DiGiorgio's labor camp. The newly striking workers were trying to retrieve some clothing and a few other possessions when six or seven armed security guards met Chavez at the camp. At gunpoint, the guards forced Chavez and two of his friends into the back of a transport truck and held then captive for several hours as the temperature hovered near one hundred degrees. The truck had no windows, only small slits in the side.

The workers were worried that Chavez and the others might suffocate and began chanting for the guards to release them. Around ten o'clock that evening the guards finally released them into the custody of several sheriff's deputies who chained the trio together and took them to San Diego.

Chavez fell asleep during the ride. He awakened upon their arrival in San Diego to find the media present: "There were all kinds of bright lights and a TV camera poking through the window taking my picture."

After a night in jail, Chavez and the others were released. The arrest was not a good idea for union opponents. When news of it spread, more farmworkers came over to the NFWA cause. The three men were later convicted of criminal trespassing and put on three years' probation.

Two weeks after the arrest, Governor Brown's investigators asked DiGiorgio to hold another election. This time officials from the American Arbitration Association would supervise it. DiGiorgio gave assurances that any employees who had gone out on strike would be allowed to vote, but then laid off 192 employees just before the election. According to Chavez, all of the fired workers were members or supporters of the NFWA. He bitterly wrote about DiGiorgio's underhanded tactics. "Their tactics were dirty," Chavez said. "They were one of the most unprincipled companies I've ever dealt with. Then they brought in Anglo high school kids to work and vote against us."

The election was scheduled for August 30. Chavez knew that if NFWA lost this time, it might be the death of the union and even of the movement. He decided it was time to combine with the AWOC to enlarge the movement, something Kircher had been imploring him to do for months. In July 1966 the membership of both unions voted to approve a merger. The new union would be called the United Farm Workers Organizing Committee, later shortened to the United Farm Workers (UFW). Its executive board named Chavez as director and Itliong as assistant director.

Most of AWOC's organizers left after the merger. Before the merger, most of the AWOC's organizers had been paid one hundred and twenty-five a week. After the merger, their pay was reduced to what Chavez's organizers made—five dollars a week plus room and board—and many of them quit.

Ross stayed on to oversee the campaigning and canvassing for the second election. He maintained detailed records on every potential voter. Each time union workers visited one they recorded any concerns and logged the information in a card file. Ross had workers go back to the voters until every question and concern was satisfactorily answered.

Chavez could hardly sleep the night before the election. Around three o'clock in the morning, he finally dozed off after reminding himself that if they lost, they would not be any worse off than when they started. After less than two hours of sleep, he got up and helped to organize a car pool so his supporters could cast their ballots. The polls stayed open until 8:00 PM. Many observers believed that the Teamsters would win. Chavez's old friend and mentor, Saul Alinsky told him: "You're going to be decimated. The Teamsters are too strong."

After the polls closed, the ballots were placed in a box that was put into the trunk of a California Highway Patrol cruiser. Representatives from DiGiorgio, the Teamsters, and the UFWOC climbed into the cruiser and sped off to San Francisco, where the ballots would be officially tallied and recorded.

Chavez stayed in Delano to await the results. He tried to remain optimistic, but prepared himself for bad news: "I was . . . making plans on what to do in case we lost, how to deal with the strikers. Then Dolores called from San Francisco," Chavez recalled.

The field workers voted for the UFWOC over the Teamsters, 530 to 331. Only twelve workers voted for "no union." It was a significant victory for the UFWOC. Among its members there was a collective feeling of joy and celebration, but Chavez was never one to rest on his laurels. It was time to move on to other challenges.

Despite recent victories, the UFWOC had won contracts for only around five thousand of California's two hundred and fifty thousand farmworkers. A few growers had raised wages without entering into a union contract, but there was still widespread exploitation. Children as young as six were employed as strikebreakers.

Chavez thought that the grape growers were the most exploitative. He decided the union's next target would be

Chavez was successful in making the boycott of California grapes into a national campaign. (Courtesy of Walter P. Reuther Library, Wayne State University)

California's biggest grape grower. Giumarra Vineyards in Bakersfield farmed over eleven thousand acres of grapes. Their workers had complained to Chavez and other union officials about wages and working conditions. Workers were paid by the quantity of suitable grapes they picked instead of by the total quantity and Giumarra kept wages low by insisting only the best grapes could be harvested.

For several months the UFWOC tried to negotiate a contract with Giumarra. It sent registered letters to company officials asking them to meet at the bargaining table but the Giumarra management ignored the letters. The company's founder, Joseph Giumarra, was staunchly anti-union.

In August 1967 the workers at Giumarra voted to go on strike and nearly two-thirds of the company's five thousand workers walked off the job during the grape harvest.

Giumarra quickly brought in strikebreakers for the harvest and began using the legal system to stymie the strike. They obtained court injunctions banning the strikers and picketers from using bullhorns and another limiting the union to using only three picketers at each entrance to a Giumarra field.

The union retaliated by calling for a nationwide boycott of Giumarra's grapes. In New York City, Mayor John Lindsay issued an executive order that forbade any city agency to buy California grapes. The mayors of Boston, Detroit, and St. Louis also ordered their purchasing agents not to buy California grapes. In other cities the union had picketers waiting when trucks filled with grapes from Giumarra arrived at the loading docks.

Under Ross's leadership, the boycott spread to four major cities—Boston, Chicago, Los Angeles, and Detroit. Union activists traveled to these and other cities and contacted different organizations, churches, labor groups and unions, civic groups, women's groups, and student groups. They also recruited picketers and solicited financial support and arranged for supporters to picket the chain stores that sold California grapes. "The heavy emphasis was placed on cracking the big chains, getting them not to handle table grapes," Ross said. "To do that, we were using the secondary boycott, asking people not to shop there until the grapes were removed. . . . More and more people were refusing to buy grapes."

Giumarra found another way to foil the spreading boycott. With the cooperation of other growers, Giumarra began shipping its grapes under other growers' labels. Now consumers and picketers did not know which brands to boycott:

> When the boycott began to make a dent, Giumarra started changing the labels. First they had six [different labels]. Then in less than sixty days they had about sixty. Soon, we were dealing with over a hundred. Although it was against the law, they were using the labels of all the California growers against us.

With the strike and boycott suddenly floundering, Chavez was forced to change his strategy. Huerta and Ross had been urging him to widen the boycott to all grape growers. It was not something he had wanted to do, but the label changing strategy used by Giumarra left him no choice. In January 1968 the UFWOC expanded the boycott to include all California table grapes.

The expansion of the boycott tested the resolve of the workers who were growing frustrated at being unemployed. Some members began to advocate violence. Chavez had to find a way to lift their sagging spirits and revitalize the union's commitment to nonviolence.

CHAPTER 9.

Fast

As the farmworkers movement grew, Chavez was finding it more difficult to stop some of his followers from engaging in acts of reprisal against the growers. Workers blew up water irrigation pumps and scattered nails across roads to flatten the tires of farm trucks and police cars. A few times arsonists destroyed some packing sheds stocked with grapes and there were reports of farmworkers beating up those suspected of spying.

Chavez was disheartened and infuriated by reports of violence against the growers. He expelled anyone he knew had participated in these acts or provoked a physical confrontation on the picket lines. Sometimes, he took away guns from farmworkers when he learned that they were carrying weapons. But even disarming farmworkers could not always stop the violence. In one instance, a worker drove his car into three growers. One of the growers suffered broken hips and the worker was sentenced to a year in jail.

Chavez's major strikes were organized against the grape growers and growing regions marked in purple.

In February 1968, union leaders held a private meeting with Chavez. They had disturbing news. The district attorney in Kern County, California was considering filing charges against union members suspected of destroying property. The district attorney would ask for long prison sentences for anyone he was able to convict.

As the leader of the boycott and the union, Chavez needed to stop the violence. But after two-and-a-half years of strikes and boycotts they had contracts with only nine growers, and morale was at a low point. This made it harder to get the rank and file of the union to reaffirm the ideal of nonviolence. Chavez said later that, "I thought that I had to bring the Movement to a halt, do something that would force them and me to deal with the whole question of violence and ourselves. We had to stop long enough to take account of what we were doing."

Chavez decided to stop eating until the violence ceased. His study of Gandhi had inspired him to go on a hunger strike. During his struggle to free India from British rule, Gandhi had engaged in periodic fasts to bring attention and support to the cause.

Chavez's fast began in private in mid-February when he quit eating solid food and sustained himself with diet soft drinks. On the fourth day, he switched to drinking water only. Then he called a meeting at the Filipino Hall to discuss his concerns.

Although he was already weak, Chavez had enough energy to chastise strikers for resorting to violence. He also criticized union organizers for not doing enough to prevent the violence and denounced the saboteurs for endangering the union's support and credibility:

> Then I talked about violence. How could they oppose the violence of the war in Vietnam, I asked, but propose that we use violence for our cause? When the Civil Rights Movement turned to violence, I said, it was the blacks who suffered, who were killed, who had their homes burned. If we turned to violence, it would be the poor who would suffer.

Workers farm in a field at Forty Acres, a labor camp outside of Delano, California, that was later turned into union headquarters. (Courtesy of Walter P. Reuther Library, Wayne State University)

Chavez concluded his remarks by announcing that he would not eat until one of two things happened—either all of the strikers would ignore him and continue to commit violent acts, or they would all decide to stop the violence. When he finished speaking he did not wait for reactions or take questions. He simply announced that he was walking back to Forty Acres, an old labor camp outside of Delano that had been turned into union headquarters.

News of his fast provoked a mixed reaction. The growers accused him of a publicity stunt, and some union members accused Chavez of trying to make himself into a martyr. But most union members supported him. For many of them, Chavez's fast called to mind the self-denial that was an important tradition in Mexican culture.

Many of his supporters worried that the union's work would cease during the fast but it had the opposite effect. As the news of it spread, thousands of farmworkers journeyed to Forty Acres to support Chavez and the UFW. They camped out and held prayer rallies and priests conducted mass while wearing vestments cut from UFW flags. Chavez's aide, Leroy Chatfield recalled:

> The irony of the fast was that it turned out to be the greatest organizing tool in the history of the labor movement—at least in this country. Workers came from every sector of California and Arizona to meet with Cesar, to talk to him about the problems of their areas. . . . Cesar had more organizing going on while he was immobilized at the Forty Acres fasting than had ever happened before in the union.

As the fast continued, members of the national news media came to Forty Acres to chronicle it. The growers watched in frustration as public sentiment shifted to the farmworkers. On the thirteenth day Chavez was forced to appear in Kern County Superior Court to face contempt charges for picketers' violations of injunctions. Giumarra had been granted injunctions limiting the number of picketers to three at each entrance to their ranch and another injunction barred strikers from standing within three hundred feet of each other. These were unacceptable to the union

Robert Kennedy and Chavez sharing a piece of bread at the end of Chavez's hunger strike in 1968. (Courtesy of Walter P. Reuther Library, Wayne State University)

and had quickly been violated. Chavez's appearance in court to answer these charges, which were seen to be the result of the company's wealth and power over the local court system, generated favorable publicity for the UFW.

Over three thousand supporters followed Chavez to the courthouse. They crowded into the hallways and held a quiet prayer vigil outside of the courtroom. Giumarra's attorneys asked the judge to remove the farmworkers, but the judge refused and Giumarra dropped the contempt charges.

After twenty-five days, Chavez ended his fast. During that time his only nourishment had been water, wafers, and some bouillon. He had lost thirty-five pounds. To celebrate its end a huge rally was held at a park in Delano. Senator Robert F. Kennedy flew in to attend and the two Catholics symbolized the ending of the fast by sharing a piece of bread blessed by a priest.

Chavez was too weak to speak to the crowd, but he wrote down his thoughts and his friend, Jim Drake, read them aloud. The remarks were brief, but they inspired the listeners to continue with the strike and with the boycott:

> Our struggle is not easy . . . Those who oppose our cause are rich and powerful, and they have many allies in high places. We are poor. Our allies are few. But we have something the rich do not own. We have our own bodies and spirits and the justice of our cause as our weapons. When we are really honest with ourselves . . . we must admit that our lives are all that really belong to us. So it is how we use our lives that determines what kind of men we are. It is my deepest belief that only by giving our lives do we find life.

Six days after Chavez ended his fast, Kennedy announced that he would seek the Democratic Party's 1968 presidential nomination. His quest for the nomination abruptly ended when he was murdered by an assassin's bullet on June 5, 1968, the night he won California's presidential primary. Kennedy's assassination was a devastating blow to Chavez and the UFW. They had hoped that they would have an ally in the White House. Now it looked more likely that the next president would be Richard Nixon, a Republican from California who had publicly opposed the grape boycott.

In November 1968, Nixon defeated the Democratic nominee, Vice President Hubert Humphrey and Chavez detected an immediate change in the attitude of the federal government toward workers' rights. Washington was more hostile to the farmworkers' strike and the boycott after Nixon became president in January 1969. For example, during his first year in office, the Department of Defense bought eleven million pounds of fresh grapes. The previous year it had bought less than seven million pounds.

The boycott and strike continued even without support from Washington. The growers began to pay an economic price. Total grape acreage declined, as did the number of growers. In August 1968, the *Wall Street Journal* reported that the strike and boycott had cost the growers nearly 20 percent of their national market. The growers seemed to agree that it was hurting them. In a lawsuit filed against the UFW, the growers' organization claimed the boycott had cost them $25 million in lost revenues.

According to one poll, seventeen million Americans were

boycotting California grapes. The boycott had expanded outside of the United States. Dock workers in several European countries refused to unload California grapes from merchant ships.

By 1969, the growers were ready to negotiate with the UFW. Chavez resisted their offer initially because their proposed contract was not much of an improvement over existing conditions. This angered some of the other UFW officials and members, and Chavez's refusal to negotiate also upset some of the AFL-CIO's top officials. But Chavez remained convinced that if the boycott kept exerting pressure on the growers, the UFW would get a better contract. If they settled too quickly, four years of sacrifice would be lost.

Although he would not admit it publicly, Chavez was growing weary of the struggle himself: "By this time we were fighting on four fronts, and each was taking a lot of manpower. There was the strike, the boycott, the legal cases and the whole propaganda front," Chavez recalled.

The first victory for the UFW came in April 1970 when three vineyards in the Coachella Valley signed a union contract. These vineyards employed about 750 workers during the peak of the harvest and produced less than 2 percent of California's total output of grapes. The growers agreed to pay the workers $1.75 an hour and an additional twenty-five cents for each box of grapes they picked. They further agreed to put ten cents for every work hour into a health and welfare fund for the workers and two cents per work hour into a fund for workers who lost their jobs because of old age or mechanization.

A poster exhorting consumers to only buy grapes harvested by union labor.
(Courtesy of Walter P. Reuther Library, Wayne State University)

The agreement with the Coachella Valley growers did not start a stampede of growers who wanted to sign union contracts. Progress was more gradual. The turning point came when the UFW signed with a grower named Karahadian. The boycott had cost Karahadian his biggest buyer when the Mayfair chain of stores decided to support it:

> When he came to us, he wanted a contract retroactive to that day that he lost Mayfair. . . . The day after he signed a contract, he sold ten thousand boxes in five hours. In three days, he emptied his cold storage. Not only that, but Union grapes with our eagle on them were selling from fifty to seventy-five cents more a box.

Once Karahadian settled, Chavez received five to ten calls a day from growers ready to sign union contracts. Many consumers continued to refuse to buy grapes that did not have the black eagle symbol of the UFW on the box. When the growers asked Chavez what they had to do to get the union label, he would say: "If you sign the contract, we'll give you the bird."

In July 1970, a group of twenty-three growers announced that they would negotiate a contract with the UFW. The group collectively produced more than 40 percent of all of the grapes grown in California. The two sides bargained for a week before they were able to reach an agreement.

On July 29, the strike officially ended. UFW workers would make $1.80 an hour with a twenty-five cent an hour raise after two years. The growers would also make the same contributions to the health and welfare fund, ten cents per work hour, and for the economic development fund, two cents per work hour, that the Coachella Valley grape growers had.

John Giumarra Jr. remarked that it was an historic victory for the workers, but he remained skeptical. "If it works well here," he said, "if this experiment in social justice as they've called it, or this revolution in agriculture—however you want to characterize it—if it works here, it can work elsewhere. But if it doesn't work here, it won't work anywhere."

Chavez at the signing of the contract that ended the strike against twenty-three grape growers in 1970. (Courtesy of Walter P. Reuther Library, Wayne State University)

Chavez reminded everyone that the union had achieved its victory because of the workers' commitment to nonviolence and their sacrifices. He also thanked the millions of people who had supported the grape boycott:

> Without the help of those millions upon millions of people who believe as we do that nonviolence is the way to struggle . . . I'm sure that we wouldn't be here today. The strikers and the people involved in this struggle sacrificed a lot, sacrificed all of their worldly possessions. Ninety-five percent of those strikers lost their homes and their cars. But I think in losing those worldly possessions they found themselves.

Again, Chavez would not get to rest on his laurels. Soon he and the other UFW leaders had to turn their focus almost to another conflict. The Teamsters Union decided to challenge the UFW by negotiating with the lettuce growers in the Salinas Valley. Almost as soon as one strike ended, another began.

CHAPTER 10.
A Strong Forest

The Teamsters Union had signed secret contracts with thirty lettuce growers in California's Salinas Valley. When Chavez learned of these contracts in July 1970 the news took him by surprise. He did not want to get into a prolonged confrontation with the powerful Teamsters Union, but he knew the much smaller UFW had to fight back. The contracts had been signed without the knowledge or consent of the farmworkers and although the workers had been excluded from the negotiations, they would have to either pay union dues to the Teamsters or be fired.

There was more at stake than which union would represent the lettuce farmworkers. This was a battle for the survival of the UFW. In 1966, when Republican Ronald Reagan had been elected governor of California, he let it be known that his sympathies were with the growers. Chavez and the UFW could not expect any help from the state government.

President Richard Nixon, who was elected in 1968, had close ties with the leadership of the Teamsters Union. (Library of Congress)

There would be no help from the federal government either. The Teamsters Union had endorsed and given financial support to Richard Nixon during the 1968 presidential campaign and Nixon had close ties with the Teamsters president, Frank Fitzsimmons.

At the end of July 1970, Chavez went to Salinas to hold a press conference and a rally to gather support for the UFW challenge to the Teamsters. He addressed the farmworkers in Spanish and the reporters in English and called on Governor Reagan to set up an election so the workers could choose whether they wanted the Teamsters or the UFW to be their union. He also read a telegram that the UFW had sent to the Grower-Shipper Association.

The telegram called for immediate negotiations with the UFW and asserted that the vast majority of the lettuce farmworkers wanted the UFW to represent them. The telegram ended with a warning to the lettuce growers: "A prompt reply will avoid the bitter conflict experienced in the Delano grape strike."

The tactics the UFW planned to use against the Teamsters and the lettuce growers were similar to those they had used against the grape growers. There would be a boycott of their product and work stoppages to decrease productivity. Chavez and other union leaders had little difficulty recruiting and organizing workers after they learned the Teamster contracts only gave them a half cent per hour pay increase.

By contrast, the leadership of the Teamsters was not interested in dealing directly with the farmworkers they

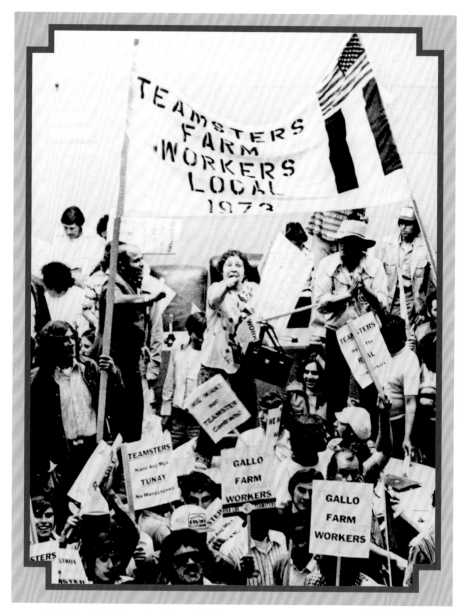

Members of the Teamsters Farm Workers protest outside a meeting of the UFW.
(Courtesy of Walter P. Reuther Library, Wayne State University)

had under contract. Einar Mohn, the director of the Western Conference of Teamsters, declared the farmworkers would not be allowed to attend any membership meetings for at least two years. Mohn even made a bigoted statement questioning the competence and intelligence of Mexican farmworkers:

> I'm not sure how effective a union can be when it is composed of Mexican Americans and Mexican nationals with temporary visas. Maybe as agriculture becomes more sophisticated . . . as jobs become more attractive to whites, then we can build a union that can have structure and that can negotiate from strength and from member participation.

The Teamsters resorted to violence. The UFW's primary attorney, Jerry Cohen, was viciously beaten while investigating a work stoppage. Cohen suffered a concussion and was hospitalized for a week. Other strikers had their car windshields shattered, while others were assaulted by Teamsters brandishing chains and baseball bats. Bomb threats were called in to the UFW offices, and Chavez received death threats.

Even though Chavez steadfastly called for nonviolence, some UFW members retaliated against the Teamsters. Three UFW members were arrested for shooting a Teamster organizer in Santa Maria, California. The man accused of the shooting had earlier been banned from a UFW picket line for assaulting someone with a lead pipe but rather than blame the attackers, Chavez held himself responsible.

Chavez faced legal problems as well as moral ones during the lettuce strike. Bud Antle, the first lettuce grower to align himself with the Teamsters, obtained a court order to stop the boycott. When Chavez refused to call it off he was charged with contempt of court and ordered to appear at a hearing that was held in Salinas in December 1970. Approximately two thousand farmworkers marched from the UFW headquarters in Salinas to the courthouse. In the crowded courtroom, Judge Gordon Campbell listened to the lawyers' arguments and then took a ten-minute recess before reading his decision. The lengthy opinion had obviously been written before he heard the arguments. It ordered Chavez jailed and added a $10,000 fine. The judge had to reduce the fine after UFW attorney Bill Carder reminded him that the maximum fine allowable by law was only five hundred dollars.

Chavez got two visits while he was in jail that focused worldwide media attention on Salinas. The first visitor was Coretta Scott King, widow of the slain civil rights leader Dr. Martin Luther King Jr. The second visitor was Ethel Kennedy, widow of Senator Robert F. Kennedy. Her visit drew a crowd of two thousand farmworkers and two anti-union demonstrators.

Twenty days after his sentencing, the California Supreme Court ordered Chavez released while his case was reviewed. Four months later, in a unanimous decision, the court ruled that Judge Campbell's injunction against the boycott was unconstitutional and that the boycott was perfectly legal. Chavez was released on Christmas Eve.

During this period the Teamsters encountered legal difficulties of their own. Ted Gonsalves, the secretary-treasurer of the Teamsters local in Modesto, had used union funds to fight the UFW workers and strikers in Salinas. Six men

Chavez (center) *and Coretta Scott King* (second from the left) *march in New York City in support of the lettuce boycott.* (Courtesy of Hulton Archive/Getty Images)

linked to Gonsalves were indicted for transporting explosives and firearms. Four of them pleaded guilty and two received prison sentences. The Teamsters had to suspend Gonsalves and put the Modesto local under a trusteeship. Gonsalves was later indicted for taking bribes.

By 1971, the Teamsters had grown tired of fighting with the UFW. Mohn announced to the lettuce growers: "We don't want the contracts. We're out."

It looked as though the UFW could finally begin negotiations with the lettuce growers, but the growers still insisted that they would not negotiate unless they called off the lettuce boycott. As a concession to the growers, Chavez called off the boycott, but after five months of negotiations the union and the growers were at an impasse. In November 1971, the negotiations ended and the boycott resumed.

During the negotiations, United States Treasury agents informed the UFW that some growers in the Delano area had paid $25,000 to hire a professional assassin to murder Chavez. The would-be assassin was arrested for another murder before he was able to fulfill his contract on Chavez, but the news forced Chavez to reluctantly go into hiding for a month. He recalled, "I didn't want to leave the union headquarters at La Paz. But I did leave in deference to the people, who were very concerned. We spent one month just wandering like Gypsies."

While pursuing an agreement with the California lettuce growers, the UFW was also deeply involved in Arizona state politics. Arizona's Republican governor, Jack Williams, signed an anti-union bill into law before the state's attorney general could review its legality. After he was asked about the farmworkers' objections to the law, Williams said: "As far as I'm concerned, these people do not exist."

Governor Williams's remark prompted Chavez to go on a twenty-four-day fast and to organize a petition drive to have Williams removed from office. Canvassers collected enough validated signatures to hold a recall vote, but Arizona's attorney general got more than sixty thousand of the signatures declared invalid because of a legal technicality. In 1974, however, the farmworkers' support helped to elect Raul Hector Castro, a Democrat more sympathetic to their cause.

Chavez and the UFW achieved several major victories during the 1970s, including the signing of a labor contract with Coca-Cola's Food Division in 1972 that gave migrant workers in the Florida citrus groves their first labor contract. Another major success was the enactment of California's Agricultural Labor Relations Act (ALRA) in 1975 that established a five-member board to ensure the rights of farmworkers to organize into unions and to engage in collective bargaining with their employers. Farmworkers finally enjoyed the same rights that many other workers had enjoyed for decades.

Despite these successes, the UFW suffered setbacks. From 1972 to 1974, its membership declined from almost sixty thousand to five thousand. In 1973 the lettuce boycott collapsed after the UFW had spent nearly three million dollars in strike funds contributed by the AFL-CIO. The UFW had been unable to regain the contracts for the lettuce farmworkers that it denied the Teamsters.

The prolonged battle between the Teamsters and the UFW ended in 1977. During the fall of 1975, the five-member board established by the ALRA supervised a statewide election in which farmworkers were asked to choose between the Teamsters and the UFW. The UFW won by a margin of 53 to30 percent, but the Teamsters remained free to organize workers in the processing and packing industries. This agreement stayed in place until 1983.

Even after coming to an agreement with the Teamsters, Chavez came under attack by farmworkers attempting to set up rival unions. He was accused of refusing to share power and of being indifferent to workers with opinions contrary to his own. Still, not even his most outspoken critics could deny that Chavez had significantly improved wages and working conditions for farmworkers with UFW contracts.

Perhaps Chavez's greatest flaw was a failure to understand that not everyone in the UFW shared his passion and commitment to the cause. During his tenure as a labor leader, Chavez never made more than $5,000 a year, the same annual wage as a farmworker at that time. After a year or two of working for such low wages, many union organizers would look for more lucrative employment. This constant turnover in personnel forced the union to spend much time training new employees.

The election of another conservative Republican to replace Jerry Brown as governor of California in 1982 contributed to the UFW's decline in membership and influence. Brown had served as governor from 1975 to 1983, and during his administration the ALRA was passed and the Agricultural Labor Relations Board (ALRB) was

During the 1980s, Chavez began speaking out about how pesticides affected farmworkers. (Courtesy of Walter P. Reuther Library, Wayne State University)

established. After George Deukmejian became governor he appointed members to the ALRB more sympathetic toward the growers than toward the farmworkers. By 1987, Chavez and the UFW had become so disgruntled with the ALRB that they asked the California legislature to reduce its funding.

In December 1987 Chavez called for another nation-wide grape boycott. This time the major issue was the pesticides that were sprayed on the grapes. Longtime consumer advocate Ralph Nader joined Chavez after a study revealed farmworkers had higher than average cancer rates. Chavez and Nader believed that the cancer rate was due to the workers' exposure to pesticides identified as potential health hazards by the Environmental Protection Agency.

To generate support and publicity for the new boycott, Chavez embarked on another fast. He was sixty-one years old, and this time his body had a harder time sustaining itself without nourishment. He fasted for thirty-six days, subsisting on water and reportedly losing thirty-three pounds while suffering from fever, cramps, and vomiting.

When Chavez ended his fast on August 21, 1988, a crowd of approximately six thousand people gathered in a field outside of Delano to pay tribute. Jesse Jackson, Ethel Kennedy, and actors Martin Sheen, Robert Blake, Emilio Estevez, and Lou Diamond Phillips came out to honor Chavez. At the end of an hour-long Mass, Ethel Kennedy handed Chavez a small piece of bread—his first solid food in just over five weeks.

For the rest of his life, Chavez worked tirelessly for the UFW and for what had come to be called La Causa, but his health was failing. On April 23, 1993, he died quietly in his sleep in San Luis, Arizona. When his death was announced, the media pressed UFW officials to speculate on the future of the union and La Causa. They issued a statement that Chavez had once made.

> Regardless of what the future holds for our union, regardless of what the future holds for farmworkers, our accomplishments cannot be undone. The consciousness and the pride that were raised by our union are alive and thriving inside millions of young Hispanics who will never work on a farm.

Chavez had wished for a simple funeral and burial, but his prominence demanded something more. A crowd

Thousands of mourners including Jesse Jackson, Edward James Olmos, and Ethel Kennedy accompanied Chavez's plain pine coffin as it was carried past the fields of Delano. (Courtesy of AFP/Getty Images)

estimated to be as large as thirty-five thousand people swarmed into Delano to pay final respects. Mourners walked in a funeral procession behind the plain pine coffin made by Chavez's brother Richard. Many strummed guitars, beat drums, sang, chanted and held up banners decorated with the UFW's black eagle emblem. Many in the crowd waved Mexican and American flags.

At the end of the march, Cardinal Mahony, the Archbishop of Los Angeles, conducted the funeral mass and read a message from Pope John Paul II. One of the thousands of mourners, a young attorney named Jose Padilla, may have best summed up Chavez's life and legacy when he spoke about a farmworker at the funeral who had reminded him of a Mexican *dicho* (proverb): "When a pine tree falls, it falls distributing millions of seeds that will one day create a stronger forest." Then Padilla added, "We are his forest."

Timeline

1927 Cesar Chavez born March 31, near Yuma, Arizona.

1937 Chavez family moves from Arizona to California hoping to earn enough money to pay their overdue property taxes.

1939 Chavezes become permanent residents of California after their Arizona farm is sold at a public auction.

1942 Finishes the eighth grade; becomes a full-time farmworker in California.

1944–
1946 Serves in the U.S. Navy during World War II.

1948 Marries Helen Fabela.

1952 Meets Fred Ross and begins working for the CSO.

1962 Resigns from the CSO to form the NFWA.

1966 Leads a 260-mile march from Sacramento to
Delano, California, to protest working
conditions for migrant farmworkers; first grape
boycott ends after the NFWA negotiates
the first contract for farmworkers in U.S. history;
NFWA merges with AWOC to become the UFW.

1968 Goes on a twenty-five-day fast to gain support
for strike against California grape growers.

1970 Union strike and boycott against grape growers
ends when UFW signs a contract with growers.

1988 Engages in a thirty-six-day fast to protest the use
of pesticides in agriculture.

1993 Dies at San Luis, Arizona, on April 23.

1994 Posthumously awarded the Presidential Medal
of Freedom by President Bill Clinton.

Sources

CHAPTER ONE: Highest Honor

p. 11, "Cesar Chavez, before his death . . . " http://
clinton6.
nara.gov/1994/08/1994-08-08-remarks-by-president-
in-medal-of-freedom-ceremony.

p. 11, "rose to become one . . . " Ibid.

p. 12, "The farmworkers who labored . . . " Ibid.

CHAPTER TWO: Arizona To California

p. 20, "On the hacienda, they were slaves . . . " Jacques
Levy, *Cesar Chavez: Autobiography of La Causa*
(New York: W.W. Norton & Company Inc., 1975), 7.

p. 23, "My dad often blindly trusted people . . . "
Ibid., 9.

p. 23, "Despite a culture . . . " Ibid., 18.

p. 23, "Although my mother opposed violence, . . . "
Ibid., 19.

p. 24, "After two or three days . . . " Susan Ferriss
and Ricardo Sandoval. *The Fight in the Fields:
Cesar Chavez and the farmworkers Union.* (New
York: Harcourt Brace & Company, 1997), 15.

p. 24, "Getting to school was a big chore . . . " Levy,
Cesar Chavez, 23.

p. 25, "Of course we bitterly resented . . . " Ibid.

p. 25, "But I could take a spanking . . . " Ibid.

p. 27, "the guy next to us... . . . " Ferriss and Sandoval,
The Fight in The Fields, 16.

p. 28, "Suddenly two cars bore down . . . " Levy, *Cesar Chavez*, 36.

p. 29, "the ad said . . . " Ibid., 40.

p. 30, "a big red tractor came to the farm..." Ibid., 41.

p. 30, "Now the tractor was at . . . " Ibid., 42.

CHAPTER THREE: Sal Si Puedes, Migrants

p. 34, "After the weigh-in . . . " Levy, *Cesar Chavez,* 48.

p. 36, "The boys slept on one side . . . " Ibid., 51.

p. 37, "We don't have food! . . . " Ibid., 52.

p. 36, "If you don't have any food . . . " Ibid.

p. 38, "probably the best . . . " Ibid., 54.

p. 38, "one of the worst winters.. . . . " Ibid.

p. 39, "There, in the middle of nothing . . . " Ibid., 56.

p. 39, "going to school without shoes.. . . . " Ibid.

p. 40, "it's not so much the money . . . " Ibid., 61.

p. 41, "About 1939, we were living in San Jose . . . " Charles Moritz, editor. *Current Biography Yearbook 1969.* (New York: H.W. Wilson Company, 1969), 87.

p. 41, "I don't know why I joined . . . " Levy, *Cesar Chavez*, 84.

p. 43, "I saw this white kid fighting . . . " Ferris and Sandoval, *The Fight in the Fields*, 33.

p. 43, "This time something told me . . . " Levy, *Cesar Chavez*, 85.

p. 44, "He (the desk sergeant) tried to scare me . . . " Ibid., 85.

p. 45, "For nearly two years . . . " Ibid., 88.

CHAPTER FOUR: An Activist's Beginnings

p. 49, "He told me about social justice, . . . " Ferris and Sandoval, *The Fight in the Fields*, 46.

p. 51, "I've been greatly influenced . . . " Levy, *Cesar Chavez,* 91-92.

p. 52, "All the experts agreed . . . " Moritz, *Current Biography Yearbook 1968.* (New York: H.W. Wilson Company, 1968), 15.

p. 53, "We never heard anything from whites unless . . . " Levy, 97.

p. 55, "I already had a plan . . . " Ibid., 98.

p. 56, "Fred did such a good job . . . " Ibid., 99.

p. 56, "At the very first meeting . . . " Ibid., 102.

p. 56, "I kept in diary in those days . . . " Ibid.

p. 57, "there were restrictions on everything . . . " Ibid., 103.

p. 58, "We had registered so many . . . " Ibid., 104.

p. 58, "I remember getting very upset . . . " Ibid., 105.

p. 59, "I was scared . . . " Ibid., 106.

p. 60, "The agents started asking me . . . " Ibid.

p. 62, "That was the gimmick. . . . " Ibid., 130.

p. 63, "We had a victory . . . " Ibid., 143.

CHAPTER FIVE: The Black Eagle Takes Flight

p. 64, "I thought of doing it alone . . . " Levy, *Cesar Chavez,* 145.

p. 68, "If CSO doesn't go . . . " Ibid., 146.

p. 68, "I just knew . . . " Ibid., 147.

p. 69, "I knew that no matter what . . . " Ibid., 157.

p. 70, "When I talked to people . . . " Ibid., 158.

p. 70-71, "It turned out to be . . . " Moritz, *Current Biography Yearbook 1969*, 88.

p. 73, "I chose the colors . . . " Levy, 173.

p. 73-74, "Because of the mobility . . . " Ibid., 176.

p. 74, "There were times of course . . . " Ibid., 178.

p. 74, "we had to do it . . . " Ibid.

p. 75, "Before our first year . . . " Ibid., 176.

CHAPTER SIX: The First Strike

p. 77, "Go see Cesar Chavez . . . " Ferris and Sandoval, 82.

p. 78, "Things are getting exciting . . . " Ibid., 83.

p. 82, "I thought that the growers were powerful . . . " Levy, 183.

p. 84, "We told them, you're going to suffer . . . " Ferris and Sandoval, 87.

p. 86, "155 years ago . . . " Levy, 184.

p. 86, "We are engaged in another struggle . . . " Ibid.

p. 86, "The strike was begun . . . " Ibid.

p. 86 "It's better to die . . . " Ferriss and Sandoval, 89.

p. 87, "There was nothing to eat . . . " Levy, 185.

CHAPTER SEVEN: "Viva La Causa!"

p. 88, "Strike! Don't work here! . . ." Ferriss and Sandoval, 91. p. 91, "Every time I got in the car . . ." Ibid., 189.

p. 89, "The growers were giving us . . . " Levy, 188.

p. 89, "Just keep talking . . . " Ibid., 187-188.

p. 91, "Finally, we made up our minds . . . " Ibid., 190.

p. 92, This is not your strike . . . " Ferriss and Sandoval, 114.

p. 93, "Sooner or later these guys . . . " Ibid.

p. 95, "All that these bills do . . . " Ibid., 115.

p. 95, "Ranchers in Delano say . . . " Ibid., 116.

p. 95, "Well, if he is on strike, . . . " Ibid.

p. 96, "The men right out there . . . " Ibid.

p. 97, "We'll stay here if it takes . . . " Levy, 208.

p. 98, "March group began with . . . " Ferriss and Sandoval, 119.

p. 99, "We are sons of the . . . " Ibid., 120.

p. 101, "The march had really caught on . . . " Levy, 212.

p. 102, "The guy said that he wants . . . " Levy, 215,

p. 103, "Oh, the hell with him! . . . " Ibid.

p. 103, "Cesar, he's got to talk . . . " Ibid.

p. 103, "No! You must be kidding. . . . " Ibid., 216.

p. 104, "It was an exciting end . . . " Ibid., 218.

CHAPTER EIGHT: Army of Growers

p. 106, "Adelina, I don't got no place for you . . . " Ferriss and Sandoval, 125.

p. 107, "I'll be damned if I'm going . . . " Levy, *Cesar Chavez* 223.

p. 108, "anything that was legal and moral, . . . " Ibid., 222.

p. 113, "There were all kinds of . . . " Ibid., 233.

p. 113, "Their tactics were dirty . . . " Ibid., 235-236.

p. 115, "You're going to be decimated . . . " Ibid., 244.

p. 115, "I was . . . making plans on what to do . . . "
Ibid., 245-246.

p. 118, "The heavy emphasis was placed . . . " Ibid., 268.

p. 119, "When the boycott began . . . " Ibid., 267.

CHAPTER NINE: Fast

p. 122, "I thought that I had to bring . . . " Levy, *Cesar Chavez,* 272.

p. 122, "Then I talked about violence . . . " Ibid., 273.

p. 124, "The irony of the fast . . . " Ferriss and Sandoval, 143.

p. 126, "Our struggle is not easy . . . " Levy, 286.

p. 128, "By this time we were fighting . . . " Ibid., 295.

p. 130, "When he came to us . . . " Ibid., 309.

p. 130, "If you sign the contract . . . " Ibid.

p. 131, "If it works well here . . . " Ferriss and Sandoval, 157.

p. 132, "Without the help of those . . . " Ibid., 157.

CHAPTER TEN: A Strong Forest

p. 135, "A prompt reply . . . " Ferriss and Sandoval, 162.

p. 137, "I'm not sure how effective . . . " Ibid., 186.

p. 140, "We don't want the contracts . . . " Ibid., 91.

p. 140, "I didn't want to leave . . . " Levy, 443.

p. 140, "As far as I'm concerned . . . " Levy, 463.

p. 145, "Regardless of what the future holds . . . "
Ferriss and Sandoval, 256.

p. 146, "When a pine tree falls . . . " Ibid., 269.

Bibliography

"Cesar's War." *Time*, March 22, 1968, 23.

Degnan, James P. "The 'Grapes of Wrath' Strike." *The Nation*, February 7, 1966, 151–154.

Dunne, John Gregory. "Strike!" *The Saturday Evening Post*, May 6, 1967, 32–36.

Ferris, Susan, and Ricardo Sandoval. *The Fight in the Fields: Cesar Chavez and the Farmworkers Movement*. New York: Harcourt Brace & Company, 1997.

Gollner, Phillip M. "Thousands in California Say Goodbye to Chavez." *New York Times*, April 30, 1993.

Levy, Jacques. *Cesar Chavez: Autobiography of La Causa*. New York: W.W. Norton & Company Inc., 1975.

Lindsey, Robert. "Cesar Chavez 66, Organizer for Union of Migrants, Dies." *New York Times*, April 24, 1993.

Moritz, Charles, ed. "Saul (David) Alinsky," In *Current Biography Yearbook 1968*. New York: H.W. Wilson and Company, 1968. 15-18.

------.ed. "Cesar (Estrada) Chavez," In *Current Biography Yearbook 1969*. New York: H.W. Wilson and Company, 1969. 86-89.

Pack, Robert. *Jerry Brown: The Philosopher Prince*. New York: Stein and Day, 1978.

"Seething Vineyards." *Newsweek*, July 8, 1968, 62.

Web sites

http://www.ufw.org
The official Web site of the United Farm Workers. Along with biographical and historical details about Cesar Chavez and UFW, the site provides information about the union's current activities.

http://www.medaloffreedom.com/CesarChavez.htm
Excellent biographical data about Chavez, as well as information about the Presidential Medal of Freedom, and information about other recipients.

http://www.pbs.org/itvs/fightfields/film.html
Information about Chavez and UFW, and details about a documentary film that covers Chavez's life.

Index